Jukebox Art

Jukebox Art

CHRIS PEARCE

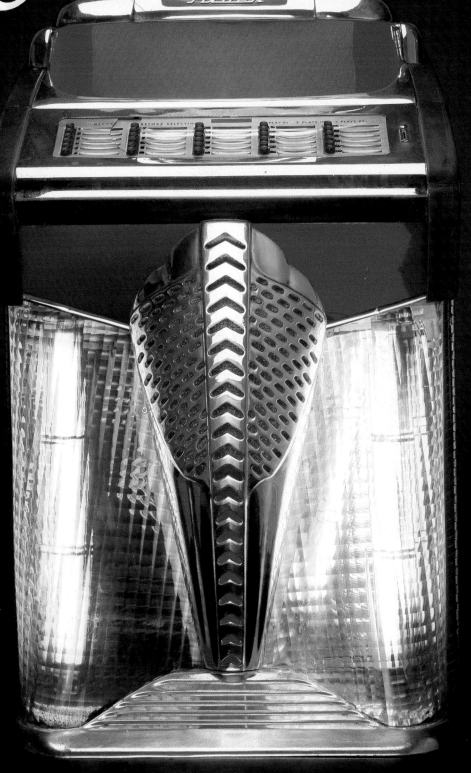

BLOSSOM

AN H.C. BLOSSOM BOOK

COPYRIGHT © 1991 H.C. BLOSSOM
ALL RIGHTS RESERVED. NO PART OF THIS PUBLICATION
MAY BE REPRODUCED, STORED IN A RETRIEVAL SYSTEM OR
TRANSMITTED IN ANY FORM BY ANY MEANS, ELECTRONIC,
MECHANICAL, PHOTOCOPYING, RECORDING OR OTHERWISE,
WITHOUT THE PERMISSION OF THE COPYRIGHT HOLDER.

ISBN 1 872532 09 8

DESIGN: IVOR CLAYDON

EDITOR: JANITA CLAMP

TYPESET IN GREAT BRITAIN BY GOODFELLOW & EGAN

PRINTED AND BOUND IN HONG KONG

H.C. BLOSSOM
6–7 WARREN MEWS
LONDON W1P 5DJ

Contents

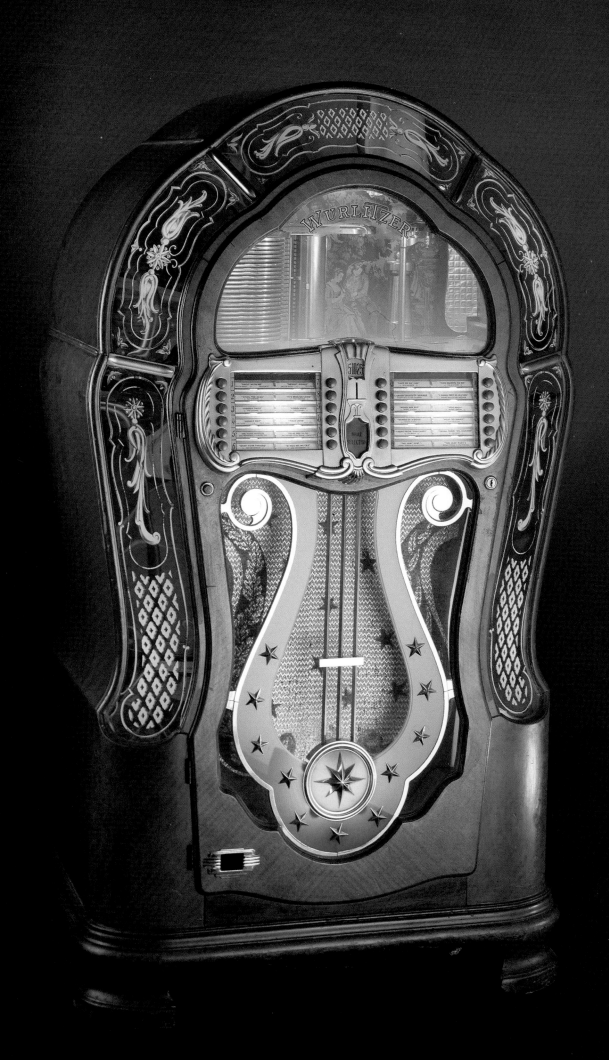

Preface

For an object which conveys such a strong image both through its physical presence and its nostalgic associations, the jukebox remains strangely enigmatic. Even though its history spans nearly a century, the jukebox achieved cult status in the 1940s and 1950s and it was this twenty year period that saw the most rapid and radical changes, driven by the need to stimulate and maintain public interest or 'play appeal'. Very often the designers succeeded, but even those machines which proved commercial failures in their day, are now appreciated as design milestones.

The enormous variety and strength of jukebox styles encompass the major design movements of the twentieth century, from art deco and streamline moderne in the 1930s through to the highly influential industrial design and Scandinavian modern in the late 1940s and taking in the influence of the automobile industry in the 1950s. However, only a handful of designers can actually be credited. The majority remain anonymous, the quest to identify them thwarted by the irretrievable loss of information that occurred when manufacturers closed down or changed hands. To compound the problem, the prevailing element of snobbery meant that the jukebox lacked the prestige which might otherwise have earned it the attention it often deserved in the design press. Even in the autobiographical review of his varied and prolific output, *Industrial Design* (Fourth Estate, 1980), Raymond Loewy features only the *United* jukebox, making no reference to the stunning styling he brought to the ill-fated *Aireon* just after the Second World War.

The history of the jukebox rests in the hands of a few giant manufacturers and these companies had the advantage of sophisticated facilities for realising design concepts into mass production. However, from time to time outsiders appeared to challenge the established hierarchy, their fresh approach and optimism reflected in adventurous styling. Technological advances also served to provide additional stimulus and extend the range of possibilities where basic materials and mechanisms were concerned.

Although there is a popular concept of jukebox style, usually epitomised by the classic *Wurlitzer* 1015, this shrine of coloured lights and brilliant, flamboyant metalwork represents only one strand in the story. With each new model the designers were faced with the dilemma of whether now was the time to stick with a winning formula or whether to upstage the competition with another radical departure.

Despite a growing interest in jukeboxes and their recent promotion to the status of collector's pieces, brought about in part by recent advertising campaigns and a current vogue for retrostyle (resulting in several modern jukeboxes being presented in 'vintage' cabinets), many models which fall outside the popular stereotypes are still awaiting a wider audience. Moreover, countless machines are losing essential elements of their contemporary design in the name of restoration. Original nickel is replated with chromium non-original and re-finishing of cabinets often results in parody rather than preservation.

The best way to appreciate the many subtleties and nuances of jukebox design is to understand its historical and social context. But however important it may be to establish the jukebox as a design classic and to preserve its original features for posterity, it is crucial not to lose sight of the fact that the jukebox is first and foremost a source of music. Even fifty years on, many machines continue to sound and look almost as good as new, a living tribute to their anonymous creators.

CHRIS PEARCE
LONDON 1991

7

Above 'Jukebox Jenny' and 'Juke Girl' show that despite the endeavours of the industry to encourage use of the more elegant name, coin-operated phonograph, Juke was by now in common parlance.

Right Wurlitzer themselves adopted the term 'Jukebox' in their patriotic World War II advertising.

Chapter One

From the Bussophone to Jukebox Jenny

According to Bill, the archetypal teenager in *The Chicago Sunday Tribune* comic strip 'Our Bill', which appeared in 1943, there was once a time, long ago, known as BJB (before juke boxes), when there were 'jive crates' and 'nickel hep houses'. To the teenagers of the 1940s and 1950s jukeboxes were so much a part of life it must have been hard to envisage a time when they were not around. Yet while this book is mainly concerned with the magic machines of these two decades, the jukebox years, it is necessary to take a brief look at the BJB period to trace the evolution of this phenomenon.

In the heady days of the late nineteenth and twentieth centuries patent offices were swamped with countless examples of human ingenuity during an epidemic of inventiveness. While many kitchen-table inventors toiled to bring the world a 'better mousetrap', others were fascinated by mechanical music devices – phonographs, player pianos, music boxes, organs, and even an electrically operated mechanical violin, the Mills *Vialano Virtuoso*. Some music boxes – which became state of the art in the late 19th century – were coin-operated, using a mechanism that handled large perforated metal discs. These magnificent devices, whose pretty, bell-like tones are so evocative of their period, are the early ancestors of the jukebox.

Recorded sound, which made the enormous leap from purely mechanical reproduction, came with Thomas Edison's 1877 discovery that sound waves could be recorded and played back from indentations in tin-foil paper. Within a year the Edison Speaking Phonograph company, to whom he had sold his invention, was producing talking machines, many of which, instead of serving the serious business and educational applications Edison had envisaged, were being used as novelties by showmen. Edison was appalled – 'I don't want the phonograph sold for amusement purposes. It is not a toy. I want it sold for business purposes only.' Unfortunately the poor sound quality emanating from the tin-foil reproducer limited the uses to which it could be put. In 1883 the problem was overcome with the invention of the wax covered cylinder which, combined with a system whereby the stylus gently followed the grooves in the wax, established the principles of the record. The inventors, Chichester Bell and Charles Tainter, formed the American Gramaphone Company in 1885 to develop and exploit their product.

The next thread in the story is the flat gramophone disc. Although there had been earlier examples, credit goes to Emile Berliner for the successful commercial exploitation of the new record which was introduced in 1893. The relative ease by which the flat gramophone platter could be handled, as well as the improved sound quality, and the public's fascination with recorded sound gave a new impetus to coin-operated phonographs. Incidentally, it is worth noting at this point that although the jukebox is a quintessential part of American life, in its early development the Europeans were just as keen to realise its potential.

In 1888 a British inventor, Charles Adams-Randall, patented the *Pariophone*, an electrical, coin-operated automatic instrument whose principles could be applied to either disc or cylinder records. Although this concept hinted at future developments in its use of electricity and the mechanised handling of records, it appears to have been the first of many such machines, which in fact sank without trace. Five years later Therese Bree, described as a 'Gentlewoman of Vienna', patented a 'Gramophone, or the like, with means for automatically changing the plates'. The inventor explained the device thus:

The apparatus has a plate-holder for receiving a given number of plates which is adjustable when the apparatus is not in action, and from which a carriage-like device removes the plate previously fixed upon it, and conveys it to the plate disc from which after the piece of music etc has been reproduced it is automatically returned to the particular compartment in the plate-holder. The device for removing the plate from the plate-holder and conveying it to the plate disc is actuated by means of the handle which serves for winding-up the clock-work, the arrangement being such that the winding-up device which is locked is released by the dropping in of a coin, so that the clock-work can be wound up, in connection wherewith the plate is brought on to the plate disc by the first movement of the handle, whereupon the clock-work is fully wound up and sets the plate disc in motion.
The device for conveying the plates to the plate disc also serves for removing the plate from the plate disc to its proper compartment in the plate-holder, and after the reproduction of the piece of music etc is ended is actuated by the winding-up crank shaft which rotates backwards whilst the clock-work runs down. The beginning of the return conveying movement is affected by the recording pin, after running through the spiral in the plate, entering a spiral line cut in the plate which runs sharply towards the centre of the plate.

Although no claims can be made for Therese Bree as the inventor of the jukebox, her patent contains all the essential kinetics: the record ('the plate') being mechanically removed from storage onto the turntable ('plate-disc'); the return mechanism actuated by the lead-off groove ('the spiral'); and the whole cycle being triggered by inserting a coin. It is certainly incongruous that the jukeboxes of post-war America had origins in turn of the century Vienna, a city and time more closely associated with Sigmund Freud and the Art Nouveau movement.

Meanwhile, other Europeans were also at work. For example, in 1913 one Franz Ackerman, a mechanic from London, patented a 'talking machine of the kind in which any one of a number of exchangeable records, preferably disc records, can

be brought into contact with a reproducer, either by manipulation of one or more handles, levers or equivalents only, or with such handles in conjunction with a coin-freed mechanism.' This device was driven by hand-wound clockwork, as was normal for contemporary gramophones.

An early attempt at an electronic jukebox, which had it gone into production would have been nearly 10 years ahead of its time, was patented by Hubert Tidswell, an engineer from Derby, in 1919. This was a 'talking machine of the automatic multiple-record type, using records of the disc type, in which any reasonable number of records may be accommodated, each separately encased or not as desired. The records may be played consecutively as arranged in the magazine, or in any desired order, and any record can be repeated any number of times in succession or otherwise. Entire control is effected electrically from any distance.'

One pioneering European invention that did go into production was the Bussophone. First patented by Cyril de Vere of Paris, in 1919, it was described as 'an improved phonograph which is capable of storing any described suitable number

*Below The novelty of its mechanism was enough to entertain the **Bussophone**'s patrons in the early twenties.*

of disc records, and comprises a selecting mechanism designed to enable any selected record to be played, all movement of this mechanism being effected without manual intervention.' The machine was envisaged either as a home entertainment unit or for commercial use, in which case it would be fitted with a coin mechanism. In 1921 de Vere's invention was incorporated in a new patent awarded to the *Societé des Phonographs Automatiques Bussoz Freres et de Vere*.

The main modification from de Vere's original concept was that instead of the turntable moving vertically and the record magazine remaining static, the improved version had a number of disc carriers that could be displaced individually by means of a rack bar, a disc selecting device, a turntable moving vertically over the whole height of the magazine, and a single crank operating the different parts of the apparatus. The mechanism was clockwork and had to be re-wound for each selection, which was made by moving a dial on the front of the cabinet. Bussoz were established manufacturers of coin-operated amusement equipment and the first Bussophone was sufficiently successful for the company to remain in the jukebox market into the 1930s. Sadly, only six of the original Bussophones are known to exist.

Despite these early European attempts, it was the Americans who pursued the development of the jukebox to the point where they can, with every justification, call it their own. There are several possible reasons for this: America appeared to be fascinated with gadgets, not only slot machines for entertainment but vending machines and an array of coin-operated devices which included, in their most extreme form, coin-operated lavatory seats and even a pay dictionary which could only be opened by inserting a coin. Furthermore, an emergent American national characteristic was the pursuit of innovation, novelty and progress. Consequently it is not surprising that two major jukebox firsts were notched up in America. Louis Glass is often accredited with being the father of the machine, a claim based on his 1889 installation of a coin-operated cylinder phonograph in the Palais Royal, San Francisco. Since there was no amplification the patron listened through one of the four tubes with which the machine was equipped. However, the connection between the event and the jukebox proper is rather nebulous, and a more credible first is the John Gabel *Automatic*

Entertainer of 1906. Although only in production for two years, this coin-operated multi-selection device paved the way for the new generation of machines which appeared in the 1920s.

The decade which ended with the Wall Street Crash in 1929 became known as the 'jazz age' and was an important jukebox decade in several respects. Prohibition saw a temporary decline in clubs and as a consequence jukebox development slowed down; when prohibition ended their fortunes took off once again. Popular music too had become an important feature of daily life, heard not only through jukeboxes but also radios and gramophones; this led to a growing demand for novelty music gadgets. There is also an interesting linguistic connection between the jazz age and the jukebox. Black slang became an increasingly popular affectation of white jazz audiences throughout this decade. Etymologists have traced the word *juke* from a corruption of the West African word *dzug*, in the Black slang of the southern states. *Dzug* meant to lead a disorderly life. In other words a juke box was originally a gramophone that entertained customers in low-life bars (juke joints) and bordellos. So unsavoury were these associations that jukebox manufacturers, sensitive to the bad press that had dogged the coin-machine industry, assiduously avoided the term, preferring the up-market image and resonant sound of 'automatic phonograph' Nevertheless the first name stuck, becoming immortalised in the 1942 films *Jukebox Jenny* and *Juke Girl*. Finally, during the war years, when the jukebox became a symbol of the American way of life, Wurlitzer capitulated and began to use the name in their advertising.

Compared to some of the early inventions described, the jukeboxes which emerged in the 1920s were surprisingly primitive. Their success lay in their use of the new technology of electric amplification, which for the first time allowed the instrument to play at sufficient volume to be considered public entertainment. Thereafter, all that was required was glamour and styling for the 'modern' jukebox to have arrived.

Chapter Two
The Big Five and the Throne of Music

The late 1920s saw a few jukeboxes come and go, as well as marking the real beginning of the modern jukebox story. The 1928 Link Autovox was an eccentric example of this transitory period. It offered a selection of 10 discs, by means of each record having its own individual turntable and tone arm. This model was short-lived though, killed off by the combination of the industrial chaos that followed the Wall Street Crash, and the emergence of a new, sophisticated jukebox industry.

Of the major jukebox manufacturers whose names dominate the golden age (generally accepted as pre-1950), three could claim a pedigree dating to the early days – Mills, Seeburg, and AMI. Of these Mills had the longest background in coin-operated entertainment, the Mills Novelty Company having been founded in 1896 to manufacture arcade equipment. Even during the jukebox years Mills was still remembered for the *Vialono*, which set a never-surpassed standard for mechanical music. It was memories of the *Vialono*'s success which meant that even after its demise at the hands of the radio, gramophone and cinema, there was a vacuum to be filled. The electrically operated mechanical violin and piano in its imposing cabinet would have been mere novelty were it not for its accurate reproduction qualities. While other player instruments relied on hand-cut music rolls, Mills had a punching device which was 'played' by the operator. In the 10 years it remained in production, from 1910–1920, some 10,000 *Vialonos* were made, earning an official designation from the US Government as 'one of the 10 greatest American inventions of the decade', and a place in the Smithsonian and Henry Ford Museums. After the *Vialono* was killed off, Mills continued to prosper with slot machines and coin-operated scales, their main lines of production. The emergence of amplified sound gave Mills the opportunity to replace the *Vialono*, and in 1926 they brought out their first jukebox. Using a large ferris wheel format in which each record was affixed to its own turntable, the first *Troubadours* were non-selective, but they were

subsequently modified. Mills continued to make ferris wheel type jukeboxes through the 1930s.

AMI (Automatic Musical Instrument Company) had a similar background in player instruments and enjoyed considerable success with coin-operated pianos until, like Mills, its products were killed by newer forms of entertainment. AMI's first jukebox was introduced in 1927, uniquely being able to play both sides of 10 records. Selection was a basic system whereby each title had its own individual coin slot. This system was retained for subsequent models, and made its last appearance in the 1936 *Top-Flight*, an appropriate name for its cabinet style, a radical departure from the basic format of its forerunners. *Top-Flight* was a classic example of 'streamline moderne' which reached its peak with the 1940 *Mills Empress*.

Seeburg, too, shared a background in mechanical music. A family business (as Mills had been) until 1956, it was founded by Justus P. Seeburg in 1902 as the J.P. Seeburg Piano Company. Seeburg had come to America as a Swedish immigrant in 1887, and had worked for piano companies before setting up on his own. Although the early days of Seeburg are remembered for its *orchestrions*, (introduced in 1910), elaborate player pianos that also featured automated drums, cymbals, violas, and wind instruments, it must be noted that in an autobiographical account of his early days, published in 1940, Seeburg claims that in 1908 the company produced an eight-record phonograph. Nevertheless, like AMI and Mills in the late 1920s, Seeburg saw the jukebox as a replacement of the

Above The **Dancemaster** *models of the thirties exemplify Mills' solid yet stylish jukeboxes.*

by then old-fashioned mechanical music.

Seeburg's first jukebox came out in 1927, but was non-selective. However, the next year two selective *Audiophones* were produced. Utilising the technology of the orchestrions, they were partly pneumatically operated, and, as with the Mills, the mechanism was a ferris wheel. However, the Wall Street Crash prematurely curtailed these developments, and Seeburg dropped jukeboxes in favour of diverse industrial products until the post-Repeal period of 1934. This interlude gave Seeburg a wide technical base which within 10 years transformed it from a piano/jukebox company into a major industrial concern.

Both Wurlitzer and Rock-ola missed out in the early days, and came into jukeboxes on the wave of Repeal. Wurlitzer's history is indirectly linked with Holcombe and Hoke who were long established manufacturers of coin-operated machines, particularly popcorn vendors. In 1926 they introduced a multiple-record, non-selective jukebox, the *Electromuse*. Although at first purely acoustic, it was almost immediately changed to electric amplification. In their employ was an ambitious young salesman, Homer E. Capehart. He was destined to become the father of the jukebox, being an irrepressible entrepreneur whose farmboy-to-senator

story was in the classic American mould. On his own initiative he acquired the right to a new changer mechanism, only to find his reward was being fired. Not long after, Holcombe and Hoke, an old-fashioned company which was content to let back-orders for the popular *Electromuse* build up instead of stepping up production, disappeared from the jukebox world.

In 1928 Capehart secured financial backing and went into production with the *Orchestrope*. Despite technical problems and a series of cliff-hanger financial adventures the *Orchestrope*, now re-designed, was heading for major success when Capehart decided to go up-market with the production of luxury domestic record players. The *Capehart* became a household name, and the elaborate installations which international millionaires, celebrities, and royalty commissioned earned a feature in *Fortune* magazine. Even though many of his customers survived the Great Depression that followed the Wall Street Crash, they did not generate sufficient sales and in 1932 Capehart was again fired, this time from his own company!

However, it was the economic climate that undermined the luxury record player market which gave the jukebox its next lease of life. Suddenly, for thousands of Americans, every cent counted. Cinema managers began to make gifts to their patrons of a piece of 'Depression glass'; the price of a ticket and temporary respite from daily care could be justified when it resulted in a colourful jug or bowl to take back home. A few coins spent listening to a jukebox or portable record was considered another budget treat. The 'New Deal' started the long haul of regeneration which was to occupy the rest of the decade, but for the jukebox the significant breakthrough was Repeal. This event which gave the green light to the two latecomers, Wurlitzer and Rock-ola, was especially welcomed by the coin-op industry, who saw Roosevelt as one of their own – in earlier times he himself had been director of a coin-op company, the Cameo Merchandising Machine Co. of New York. Anticipating its announcement, the city of Chicago provisionally granted over 700 liquor licences, with over 2,000 pending. Decorators became busy refurbishing bars, restaurants and clubs for the new era.

The next big name on the scene was Wurlitzer. In fact the music company Wurlitzer had a long history. Rudolph Wurlitzer, a German emigrant, secured a lucrative contract for the supply of

Above The Wurlitzer **Model** 412 *of 1936 continued to be sold until 1938. The direct descendant of the 1934 P. 10, it epitomises the classic look of first generation Wurlitzers.*

Right Repeal brought a return to social life which had suffered through the dry years of prohibition, giving the jukebox the focal role it had been waiting for.

bugles and drums to the military in 1860, within months of becoming an American citizen. By the end of the Civil War Wurlitzer was the biggest supplier of these instruments in America, a base from which the company expanded into a major retail music business, the first Wurlitzer piano appearing in 1880. By the end of the nineteenth century Wurlitzer were marketing a coin-operated music box – *The Regina* (1896) – and a coin-operated player piano – the *Tonophone* (1899). In 1910 Wurlitzer added the Hope-Jones Organ Company to its many musical concerns, and from this developed the famous M*ighty* W*urlitzer* cinema organ. Like AMI and Seeburg Wurlitzer produced orchestrions and player instruments, and similarly suffered when sales began to fall. Even the M*ighty* W*urlitzer* was threatened by the arrival of the talkies, as cinemas went over to amplified sound. It was almost as if fate brought Farny Wurlitzer (Rudolph's son who became the company president in 1932) and Capehart together. Capehart, an indefatigable entrepreneur, had acquired the rights to a small jukebox manufacturer Simplex, whose jukebox called the *Debutante* featured a sophisticated changer mechanism. Farny wanted to diversify into new products and was convinced by the persuasive Capehart that Repeal would bring jukeboxes to the fore. In 1933 Wurlitzer marketed the *Debutante* under its original name, and the next year renamed it the P 10.

This 10-selection machine was the first Wurlitzer marketed under the name which was to become a generic term for the jukebox. For the formative years the company's history was in Capehart's guiding hands, because not only did Farny take him on as part of the *Debutante* deal, but he rose to the

position of vice-president and general sales manager of the jukebox division. In 1940, however, Capehart resigned from Wurlitzer, pursuing other interests, notably politics.

Rock-ola had appeared on the scene in 1935. Although lacking the musical experience of the

Rock-ola adopted a pragmatic approach to Jukebox styling. By their own admission, they simply looked at what was going on around them — at first finding inspiration from radio cabinets — and adapted these to their designs.

other jukebox companies, there was a solid background of coin-operated scales, pintables, and a variety of games that gave the company a good foundation in manufacturing and marketing. Within its first jukebox years, Rock-ola had almost caught up with the competition. Then in 1936, they scored a major coup by providing a jukebox for the new Cunard luxury liner, the *Queen Mary*. According to a contemporary press report this happened at two hours notice: as there was no time to organise. a truck a taxi had to be hired. The report continued . . . 'great secrecy necessarily had to surround this move. Due to the tremendous interest by the public in this wonderful ship a special squad of private detectives had to assist the regular police department in clearing the way so that the taxi carrying the *Rock-ola Multi Selector* could reach the decks of the *Queen Mary*. After some manoeuvres representatives of Rock-ola's products dashed through the crowd and reached their goal, the mighty *Queen Mary*.' It seems strange that a

company which could not find a truck nevertheless managed to rustle up a squad of private detectives at such short notice. Perhaps this dramatic event, with a taxi cab bearing a case prominently marked *Rock-ola Multi Selector* was in fact a publicity stunt. Rock-ola capitalised on this prestigious deal by shortly afterwards bringing out a pintable called the *Queen Mary* bearing a picture of the ship on the play field.

The competition between the four main manufacturers, resulted in a design and marketing war which produced an exciting array of jukeboxes. Wurlitzer, AMI, and Rock-ola had the advantage of a record changer that served them through the 1940s, and although Mills continued with the ferris wheel until 1939 Seeburg abandoned it in favour of the short-lived 'Wilcox' mechanism, whereby a stack of interspaced records was played by a vertically traversing tone arm. Seeburg probably adopted this as a stop-gap measure, for it only appeared in the two selectophone models of 1934 and 1935. Thereafter apart from a brief experiment utilising a hybrid Wurlitzer mechanism, the Seeburg used the Friborg sliding tray changer until 1948.

A new generation of jukeboxes appeared in 1936. Luxury was now the key word in styling, with great emphasis on beautifully veneered cabinets. A contemporary article noted that:

Responding to the demand for more machines, manufacturers have been turning out new models of greater attractiveness than ever before. Modernity has arrived. Streamlines, in design and colour, are the rule of the day. Gone is the old-fashioned machine which was almost forbidding in its solitary majesty. Usually finished in dark wood, these old machines repelled rather than invited patronage. Now, all that is changed. Light cabinet work, finishes resembling natural wood such as can be seen in all modern-type furniture are favourites. The cabinets of the newer models are attractive in the very patterns of the alternating light and dark woods, while additional decoration is often used to carry out the general idea.

Above Seeburg were dedicated to pure engineering but they also excelled as stylists, bringing to their jukeboxes the latest art deco lines, and fine veneers.

The five Seeburg models of 1936 are representative of this cabinet treatment. The excellent *C* and *D* (both identical cabinets) are outstanding examples of American art deco. An awareness of modern design was destined to distinguish Seeburg from the other main manufacturers. This can be seen as symptomatic of the company's high ideals, which they conveyed in the statement 'We are definitely committed to a permanent "uplift" movement, politically, morally, economically and socially.' Proof that this applied to the company's labour relations was evident on one occasion during the war when the workforce voluntarily surrendered their vaca-tion time to undertake an emergency rush job.

Seeburg set the pace in terms of style and technology, being particularly noted for high quality sound. A rural radio DJ, who was also a jukebox operator, used a Seeburg as the station's record player. He is quoted as saying . . .

In between groups of recordings I make the following announcement. "You have been listening to a recording on a Seeburg phonograph. Listen to a Seeburg in your favorite drug store, tavern or restaurant." Since this district is strictly an agricultural community the [major use] of my phonographs occurs on Saturdays and Sundays, when the farmers visit the small towns to do their weekly shopping. By means of my radio station I have been able to contact these people in their homes and have successfully brought to their attention the fact that they can get more enjoyment out of their visits to town by spending part of their recreation time listening to the world's best music on a Seeburg phonograph.

*Below The Seeburg **Model J** of 1937 represents the climax of pre-light-up styling. Its fine veneer work, including ebony, enhanced its distinctive asymmetrical form.*

Below Electrification brought the jukebox to rural backwaters, away from the city lights and busy bars featured by manufacturers in their advertising material.

Bing Crosby ('King of the jukeboxes') as well as Benny Goodman and Cab Calloway were featured in Wurlitzer's advertisements for the Model 24. The top names in music favoured jukeboxes for promoting their records, but the musicians' union saw them as a threat to live music.

This cameo conjures up a useful picture of rural American life before World War II, for outside the large industrial centres and towns were communities which, in some areas, were quite isolated.

An important part of Roosevelt's policies to end the recession was the rural electrification programme. Mains-powered radios were a recent innovation, being introduced only in 1927, and they encouraged the spread of greater political and social awareness. Popular radio characters such as Kate Smith (the voice of America), Amos n' Andy and little Orphan Annie could now be heard in every home. Also, radio opened up opportunities for advertising (becoming a major marketing tool) and politics (with Roosevelt's intimate 'fireside chats' to the nation). A further effect of the electrification programme was the spread of the jukebox. A mid-west operator of the time relates how . . .

After the linesmen have left and current is available to what were formerly considered backwoods areas a complete new life comes into being in the activities of the inhabitants. Amusements previously denied to them, such as electrically operated amusement devices and electrical appliances of all types are eagerly accepted by the many families. Naturally, the small cross-roads, hamlets and villages have taken a new lease of life

and are becoming centres of entertainment. In establishing my routes of coin-operated phonographs I have found it well worthwhile to follow rural electrification with my Seeburg instruments.

The spread of the jukebox (by 1938 there were an estimated 300,000 in use across America) was a major factor in reversing the fortunes of the record industry, which had been hurt by the growth of radio. From the peak sales of approximately 110 million discs per annum in the 1920s the figure dropped by about ninety percent in the early 1930s. However, by the end of the decade disc sales were up again to 33 million.

Although many musicians favoured the influence of the jukebox (band leaders Tommy Dorsey, Glenn Miller and Cab Calloway amongst others endorsing Wurlitzer, while Bing Crosby was to be dubbed the 'King of the Jukeboxes') others were actively antagonistic, not only because their livelihoods were threatened as phonographs ousted live bands, but because they received no royalties from the number of times a record was heard on a jukebox. The president of the Chicago Federation of musicians, James Caesar Petrillo, was a particularly virulent enemy of the jukebox. One Texas jukebox operator calculated that as the number of jukeboxes in his area was almost the same as the number of

registered musicians, the effect of removing juke-boxes in favour of live music would logically result in full employment for the musicians, only if they were prepared to work as one-man bands. In 1938 the National Phonograph Network was formed to exploit the popularity of the jukebox. It argued that the jukebox, like the radio could be an advertising medium. Specially recorded discs by leading musicians featured an advertising message of no more than 25 words. It was thought that jukebox advertising would be particularly useful for liquor, which was banned from radio. And then, at this controversial stage in the history of the jukebox, it underwent a radical design change.

With the exception of the industrial design image of the AMI Top Flight, jukebox styling now owed more to furniture design than to any technological inspiration; this is a normal occurrence when a new mechanical device has yet to establish its identity. For instance there are clear links between the 1936-37 jukeboxes and John Vassos' design for the 1938 RCA television. What was lacking though, was glamour and visual entertainment. By subsequently introducing these features into their machines, the jukebox designers were among the earliest exponents of industrial-style obsolescence, which had hitherto been the monopoly of the fashion industry. The implication was that each year there would be an identifiably different look, a trend that became the main feature of American consumer styling. As well as generating and constantly stimulating interest in the jukebox, these style changes increased the spread of jukeboxes as a cycle of change came about, each new model displacing its predecessor, which in turn could be used in a site which may not previously have been considered profitable. A consequence of growing sales was that by 1940 Wurlitzer in particular was concerned that the growth in the quantity of secondhand machines could adversely affect sales of new equipment. The company therefore began selling the idea of its exotic new models by appealing to the purchaser's vanity.

Nothing upset the coin-operated machine industry as much as its poor status in the community. Despite the massive industrial complexes that made the machines, despite the household names of Wurlitzer, Mills, and Seeburg, there still lurked a seedy public image of novelty arcades, speakeasies and, at worst, gangsters and racketeers. Being coin-operated, jukeboxes were tarnished through

Gabel enhanced their cabinet with colour in the appropriately named **Rainbow** *of 1938. Added appeal was given to the visible mechanism through extensive chrome plating.*

association with slot machines, which were a prime target for sensationalism, as shown in this press release for the 1937 Paramount movie *King of Gamblers*. It 'takes audiences right into the heart of the slot machine racket ... a sizzling piece of screen entertainment ripped raw from the secret annals of organised crime ... for a take of more than $150,000,000 a year the overlords who run this racket will do anything, even murder.' In addition there were real-life stories of 'heavy' techniques employed to obtain and defend jukebox sites, and it seemed that every enhancement of the jukebox image such as Rock-Ola's *Queen Mary* installation, was counteracted by a hostile press, with the *Chicago Herald Tribune* being particularly antagonistic.

To make matters worse there was an element within the jukebox business whose activities played into the critics' hands. The use of smutty potentially offensive records featuring sexual innuendo horrified the trade and the white middle-class establishment.

... the few extra dollars which these records bring in on some locations will be more than offset by

Above Seeburg's advertising stressed that illumination enhanced the jukebox experience, thus resulting in more money being put into the machine – an important selling point when mean-spirited sites would query the extra running costs!

Above (centre) Wurlitzer's Model 24 was their first featuring back-lit translucent phenolic plastics. In recognition of its unique status, Wurlitzer made an exception to the rule of jukebox designers remaining anonymous and credited Paul Fuller.

Above (right) As the styling wars between the manufacturers intensified, Wurlitzer added a new feature to their illuminated plastics; turning cylinders which enlivened the jukebox with the novelty of animation.

the bad influence they will create in the minds of the public who will come to look upon the coin-operated phones as equipment featuring only a low type of entertainment . . . in some territories operators are being forced against their will to turn to smut discs in order to hold their locations, as some members of the evil minority have been successful in winning a few locations by featuring records of this type.

Wurlitzer's advertising campaign emphasised the high status an operator would acquire through its jukeboxes. Publicity material depicted exaggerated aristocratic figures admiring the jukebox, precisely the kind of people Capehart hoped to attract when he turned his back on jukeboxes in favour of home units. The message was explicit – this was the social strata in which a Wurlitzer owner was to be found. And just in case there was temptation to hold onto old equipment a generous trade-in allowance was offered. Wurlitzer backed up their pledge that old machines would not re-appear on the market with publicity photographs of old equipment being smashed.

The era of the new glamour jukebox was heralded by the light-up jukeboxes of Seeburg, AMI, and Wurlitzer, which dominated the trade show in January 1938. Although illumination had always been a feature of the jukebox, the recent develop-

ment of translucent phenolic-resin plastic allowed the cabinets to be opened up with back-illuminated panels of colour. AMI's *Streamliner* matched a style change with the new technology of push-button selection. A further innovation was that the illuminated bar-style buttons also served as title displays, a device they used again in the *Singing Towers*, and which Seeburg adapted for their post-war 'Trashcan' series.

Seeburg brought out three light-up models, the *Concert Grand*, the *Regal*, and the *Gem*, which combined the new illumination with classic Deco-styled wooden cabinets. Rock-ola's *Monarch*, *Windsor* and *Ambassador* jukeboxes were alone amongst the major manufacturers' machines in not offering light-up cabinets, although the top-of-the-range *Monarch* did feature a kinetic illuminated front grill. David Roccola, hinting that he too was working on the light-up concept, stated 'The ideas of our creative men must remain *sub rosa* until they are tried and proved, hence the market may be potential until the distribution of the machine and the promotional program are geared to meet public demand.'

Why should they stay home?

Above The 'Jive Crate', 'Nickel Hep House', or, more simply, the 'jukebox' became a social focal point for that new phenomenon of forties America, the teenager. It was to be the teenagers and their music which would ensure the jukebox its place in the social history of the fifties.

Left The massive chain-driven ferris wheel of the Mills mechanism served the company well during their early years as jukebox manufacturers. Mills products were characterised by top quality engineering, but they also produced some outstanding art deco Jukeboxes.

Right In contrast with the **Model 412** of the same year, Wurlitzer's 1936 **Model 312** featured art deco styling.

GET THE BEST SPOTS!

WURLITZER-SIMPLEX

GETS and HOLDS the BEST LOCATIONS

Whenever demonstrated to location owners, the magnificent tone of the Wurlitzer-Simplex meets with instant approval—results in an immediate installation. Wherever installed, it assures permanent satisfaction—perpetual big income for operators and location owners alike. Experienced operators will tell you—to get and hold the best spots, operate the finest automatic phonograph on the market. That's Wurlitzer-Simplex. Find out if there is room for another Wurlitzer-Simplex operator in your locality. Mail the coupon.

THE RUDOLPH WURLITZER CO., NORTH TONAWANDA, N. Y.

THE RUDOLPH WURLITZER COMPANY
NORTH TONAWANDA, N. Y.

Light-up cabinets transformed the whole concept of what a jukebox should be, and the immediate effect was a deluge of modernisation kits of varying qualities.

The most important new jukebox for 1938 was the Wurlitzer Model 24, the first in a series of machines that would give Wurlitzer market dominance for the next 10 years. Perhaps in anticipation of this fact Wurlitzer credited the designer, Paul Fuller. This was an unprecedented honour because manufacturers normally kept the designer's name anonymous. The Model 24 was almost immediately upstaged by two successors, the Model 500 and the economy version 600, both introduced in 1938/39. Distinguished by the first use of elaborate plated decorative metalwork, which would become another feature of Wurlitzer, both models showed that the company (unlike Rock-ola) was allowing

the design department to lead the way.

Another new element of jukebox design came with the 500 – zebra turning cylinders which gave a flickering effect to the lighted pilasters. Meanwhile the 1939 Seeburgs continued the same illuminated look from the previous year with three new models, the Mayfair, Casino, and Plaza. The range was extended with two further machines, the Classic and the Vogue, whose sculpted, round-shouldered, full-

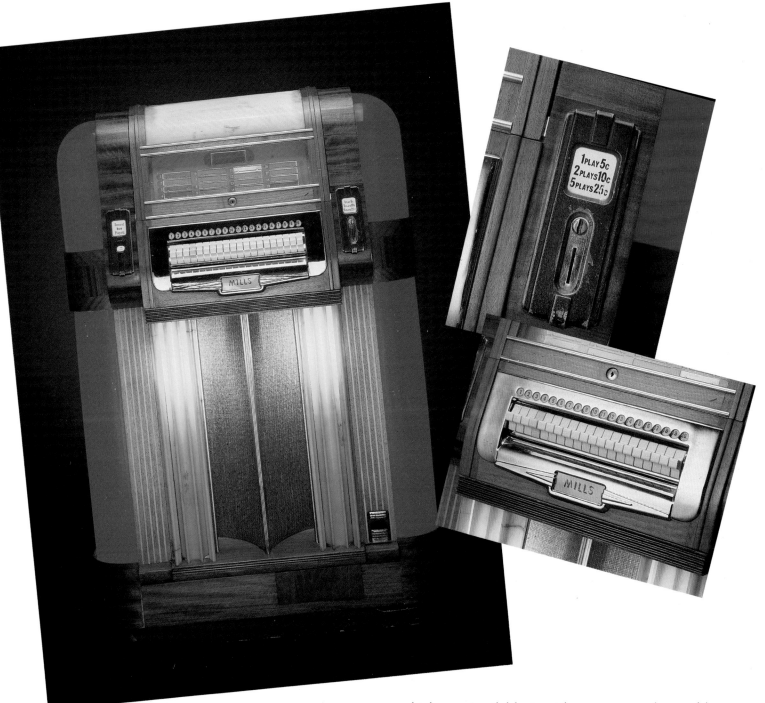

The Mills Throne of Music is one of the most imposing of the early light-ups. Elaborate veneer work adds further decorative appeal to the cabinet.

length pilastered look was further developed in the 1940 range. Rock-ola came out with the first of the luxury light-up series, which was complemented by an economy model as well as a 'counter-top', but the most spectacular newcomer to the light-up range was the Mills' *Throne of Music*.

This complete switch from the wooden-cabinet machines of the 1930s featured large light-up plastics set in an exotic veneered case. The changer mechanism was a modified version of Rock-olas'. The trend towards a varied range of jukeboxes meant the *Throne* was joined in 1940 by the *Empress*,

which was available in either a veneered or gold painted cabinet. Although slightly smaller than the *Throne*, it had the identical mechanism and sound system. Ironically while Mills regarded the *Empress* as the lesser of the two machines, it is now highly appreciated for its strong streamline moderne design, reminiscent of contemporary locomotives.

The *Empress* was styled by the Chicago industrial design and marketing consultants Magnan and Eckland, who after the war were put in charge of AMI's marketing.

The 1940 AMI jukebox is another classic of period design. The *Singing Towers*, as the name implies, was a tall machine whose style echoes skyscraper architecture, its height necessitated by having a top-mounted speaker, the theory being

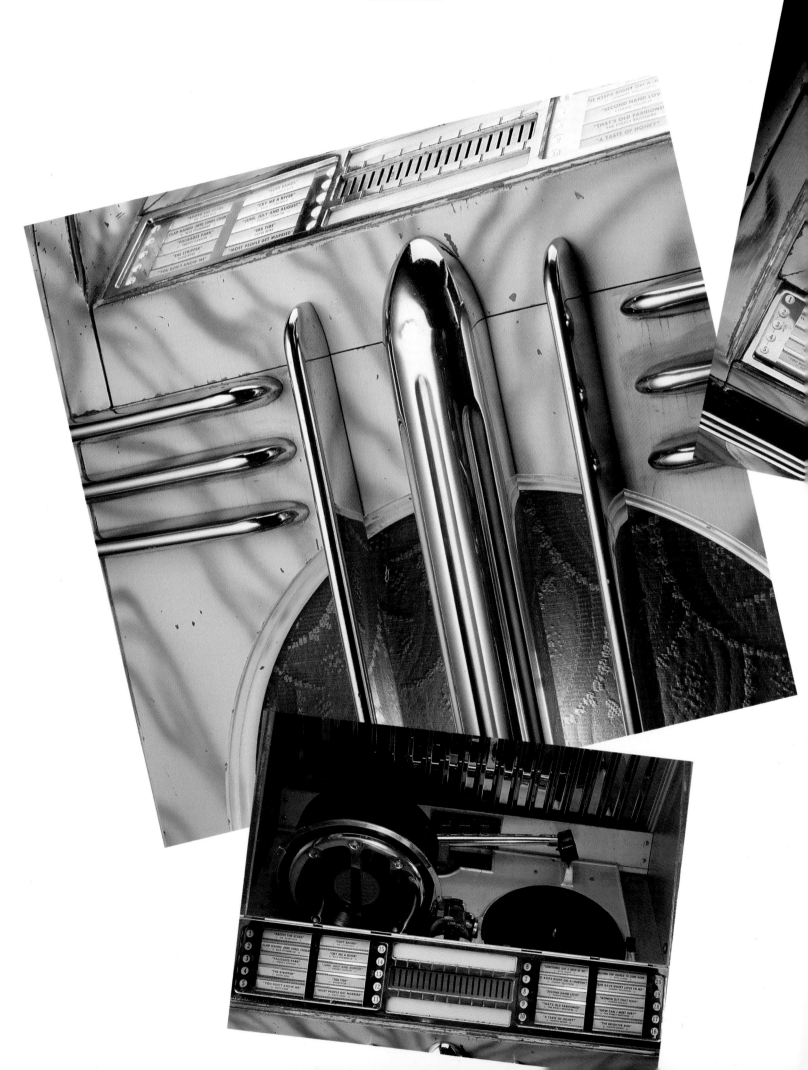

*Top Flight pioneered high tech jukebox styling with its use of the
clean lines of the 'streamline' look which was in vogue with
industrial designers. The changer mechanism was in full view,
in accordance with a major trend in jukebox design which
considered that seeing the record being played was an essential
part of the performance given by the machine.*

Above *Although the streamliner pre-dates the 'light-up' era , its use of architectural light fittings to illuminate the massive speaker, as well as reflective light bathing the mechanism is a foretaste of later jukebox design.*

Right *As neither decorative metalwork nor illuminated plastics were in use at that time, the cabinet of the Mills **Dancemaster** relied on decorative veneer to lend an air of luxury.*

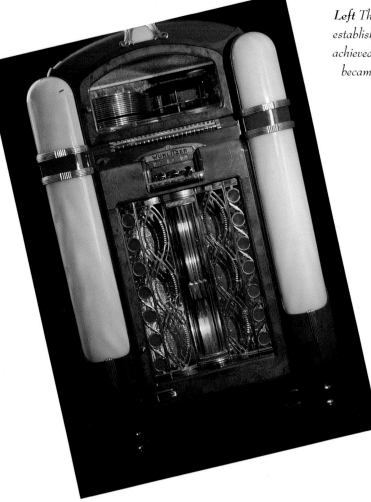

*Left The **Model 800** was the first grand Wurlitzer. Having established the precedent of adding new features, Paul Fuller achieved another first with the use of the 'bubble tubes' which became a decorative element in several successive models.*

Above In their drive to elevate its image, and by implication, the social standing of the operator, Wurlitzer's publicity pictures featured elegant, high society characters enjoying the jukebox.

*Above AMI's special position as exempt from wartime restrictions made the **Singing Towers** a welcome link with home for American troops in combat zones.*

this would produce better sound projection. Unusually for this age of plastics the light-up panels and top dome were made of faceted glass. This was quite an advantage because this wood and glass cabinet did not use prime materials needed for the war effort, so AMI did not suffer the restrictions that affected other manufacturers from 1942. In fact AMI was awarded priority status, and continued manufacturing Singing Towers through the war years for the entertainment of the forces. These jukeboxes feature regularly in photographs of American troops abroad, and so determined was AMI to put its machines 'in action' that it even devised special packing to float the jukeboxes to GI's on isolated islands, where the water was not deep enough for large ships to dock.

The two-year period leading up to American involvement in World War II was the peak of jukebox glamour. Wurlitzer brought out another paired set, the grand Model 800 and the smaller 700. Like the 500, the 800 had flickering zebra pilasters, this time with moving colour. The new innovation

was bubble tubes set in the front grille. These 'dancing bubbles' became a popular Wurlitzer feature, and indeed Wurlitzer is the only company ever to use them. These tubes are not, as is sometimes assumed, operated by air pressure, instead they contain a liquid chemical which requires only slight heating to reach its very low boiling point.

The jukebox trade went into 1940 with a formid-

Above Bing Crosby did not share his union's views on the jukebox, but then his records were always on the trade's favourites play lists. The Wurlitzer 750 featured bubble tubes but was otherwise a toning down of the opulent look.

able variety of machines to woo the public. The only setback was the election of James Petrillo, scourge of the jukebox, as president of the American Federation of Musicians. Now with national power, Petrillo set about fulfilling the mission he had begun when he was president of the Chicago union – to ban records from jukeboxes. Although he eventually succeeded in imposing a total recording ban in 1942, this was lifted by President Roosevelt who intervened on the basis that records were essential for high morale.

The year 1941 saw further classics from Paul Fuller's studio, with three major machines (not including variations, a counter model, and extension speakers) each distinctly different. The *750* was a compact and understated machine, unique for its wooden grill rather than the ornate metal version which characterised Wurlitzer. Even more unusual was its companion model, the *780*, the first Retro style jukebox. In a bid to extend the jukebox market, this machine had an ultra-conservative eighteenth-century look, with a wooden cabinet to appeal to traditional restaurants. The front grill was shaped like a wagon wheel, echoing the design of a light-fitting, popular at the time in establishments striving for a 'homely' look. The American heritage look was further accentuated by a patchwork-look grill cloth. The result was a commercial flop, partly because the industry had been very successful suggesting that jukeboxes should be colourful and exciting. The extreme example of what amounted to a theatrical experience was the Wurlitzer *850*, which used every decorative device known, and then added a new one, polarised light.

Paul Fuller applied the same styling elements that characterised Wurlitzer's full-size jukeboxes to the counter top models. The Model 41 above was the economy model for 1940, the stylish 71 below being the de-luxe version.

Above The Peacock (Model 850) was the climax of Wurlitzer's policy of adding new features, with Paul Fuller's use of polarising filters giving subtle animation to the centre panel.

Below The smaller **Model 600** lacked turning cylinders and was offered as the economy version. Nevertheless its cast, decorative metalwork still gave it a more luxurious look than its competitors.

Right Being too small to feature a live band was no longer a disadvantage, thanks to Wurlitzer, whose jukeboxes brought the sounds of Bing to even the humblest establishment.

Seeburg did not attempt to emulate Wurlitzer's extravagant styling, preferring instead to concentrate on superior engineering and technical development. Despite this, their cabinet designs were always distinctive and most of them, such as the Hi-Tones (below), are considered classics.

This magnificent machine was the biggest made in the USA (the later, aptly-named, Belgium-made Goliath did overshadow it). And its scale gave full scope to Paul Fuller's flair for decoration, involving festoons and flourishes of metal scrollwork. Besides the massive back-lit plastics, the cabinet featured as its focal point a delicate translucent panel depicting peacocks. Filtered polarised light moving behind the panel produced the effect of ever-changing iridescent colour. Even if it had been artistically possible to apply this grandiose style to new models, the war restrictions on materials announced at the end of the year would have made it impossible. Consequently the *Peacock* now has a place in history as the pinnacle of unfettered jukebox luxury. In 1942 Fuller had to do without decorative metalwork. Nevertheless, the *950*, with its elegant lines, subtly lit mirror front depicting leaping ibexes, and top arch plastics showing a decorative Pan figure, had a quieter but equally powerful beauty.

No other jukebox company took the same path as Wurlitzer in terms of style. Seeburg preferred to pursue technological development, which in the 1950s would eventually enable it to usurp Wurlitzer. Like Rock-ola and Mills, Seeburg also had many manufacturing activities outside the production of jukeboxes. Their last pre-war models took a new direction in styling, with the 1941 and 1942 Hi-Tones anticipating the cylindrical look of the post-war 'Trashcan' P146 series. At this time Seeburg was already working on a revolutionary new mechanism and, like much of American industry, already was engaged in government work in anticipation of war.

Rock-ola's last pre-war jukeboxes, the 1942 Premier, President, and Commando models, were a limited production with material restrictions demanding the use of glass instead of plastic, and a minimum of metalwork on the cabinet. Nevertheless these tall, stylish machines, like their contemporaries, represent the state of the art 1940s jukebox, for although the coming war years gave the jukebox its special place in the hearts of Americans, never again would the jukebox industry produce designs of such assurance.

*The Rock-ola **Premier**, **President** and **Commando** were a trio of similarly-styled jukeboxes, characterised by a minimum use of plastic due to materials restrictions and top-mounted speakers which dictated their height.*

The aptly named **Goliath** is the biggest jukebox ever made. Constructed by the Bartholemew Company of Belgium, its art deco look is an anachronism, for it dates from the 1950s. The **Goliath** has a rather bizarre background – Bartholemew were originally organ builders who supplied their instruments to bars and cafes. With the influence of American style on post-war Europe, including the appearance of Jukeboxes, the demand for organs tailed off and the company, showing remarkable determination, set about building jukeboxes. Utilising organ construction techniques, little of the pneumatically operated mechanism is made of metal. A radio set behind a glass panel was incorporated to supplement the music. This example is believed to be the last one made, a stereo model, and dates from circa 1959.

Chapter Three
Romance, Profit, and Turmoil

By 1941 the jukebox manufacturers, like many other American industrialists, were aware that they may have to switch exclusively to war production. In fact some had already done so, with Mills producing military hardware for the British. Deeming the word 'Novelty' in the company name inappropriate to the war products that its three massive Chicago factories were making, they eventually dropped it. Soon after, in 1943, the company changed its name to Mills Industries Inc. The owner, Fred Mills, explained. . . .

For several years before we went 100 per cent into war work we had expanded our manufacturing organisation so that it was producing heavy equipment in soft drink dispensing machinery, refrigeration compressors, air conditioning equipment, ice-cream freezers, motion picture projectors. Dealing in these lines continually suggested that we change our name. The word 'Novelty' had come into the name when the company was established by my father, Herbert S. Mills in 1889. That was the arcade era in America, and the word 'Novelty' then meant any machine that furnished arcade equipment. From now on, all of our war manufacturing will proceed under our new name.

By 1942 the jukebox was firmly established as part of the American social scene!

was at this time that America fell in love with the jukebox, which became a focal point for the high-pressure 'live for the moment' philosophy. A contemporary press report encapsulates the mood of the time. . . .

In an amusement spot some weeks ago, a Marine and a girl, strangers to each other, met in front of a phonograph, and argued over who should drop the coin first. That settled, they proceeded to fall in love. He was leaving soon so they decided to get married. 'What better place than where we first met?' they said. And so they took the vows right in front of that same music box. She wore the same slacks and white waist she'd worn that fatal day. The ceremony was performed whilst discs played tunes appropriate to the occasion, including Bing's 'Ave Maria'.

With the coin-machine industry basking in the glow of public approval, it appeared that the worst of unfavourable publicity was over. The industry could point with pride to its contribution to the war effort, with the major manufacturers gaining 'E' awards, and even the smallest operator backing the Red Cross and War Bonds drive. War work was pumping money into the economy and with millions of women now in full-time employment, financial emancipation was starting to change the social status-quo.

Women were also becoming involved in the jukebox business, some running companies whose male workforce was away fighting, others taking on the mechanical side such as the Minneapolis book keeper who in 1943, under the heading 'Feminine touch now being used on Music Boxes' was described as: 'having given up ledgers and balances to take up maintenance of a music route. She makes the daily rounds, changing records, making collections and doing repairs.'

Every jukebox that could be made to work was back in business, with many authorities having to impose a curfew to ensure that local residents managed to get some sleep! And abroad, the jukeboxes sent out to the American forces began the spread of American culture which characterised the late 1940s and 1950s. This was the time for the industry to wave the flag, and it did. According to a 1942 trade press article – 'We of the Coin Machine industry have maintained that nothing is more purely American than coin-operated machines.

*Below and overleaf Wurlitzer were unique in being able to offer a 'new' jukebox, the **Victory**, for civilian use during the war years.*

Right Shryvers were one of several wired music systems on offer. Their distinctively styled Multiphone acted as a jukebox substitute, bringing glamour, as well as music, to its locations.

They were born and raised in this country. Until we made them no other part of the world had even thought of them. They were invented, built, sold and zoomed into popularity by Americans.'

Besides establishing the jukebox, the war had other effects which influenced post-war industrial development. With the younger men serving in the armed forces, the older generation were temporarily in charge of trade, a large proportion planning to retire after hostilities ceased. Consequently the new era of trade would largely be in the hands of a younger generation eager for change. Part of that change involved recent developments in electronics, plastics and metallurgy, which prompted a brief, if unrealistic, vision of the future that owed more to science fiction than fact. As Raymond Loewy said, 'Every writer with an extra sheet of paper in his typewriter has dashed off a tale of the "dream world of the future", more because he knew that such a story would make good reading than because it bears any relation to fact.' There was no doubt that the jukebox explosion would continue after the war and that the next generation would be very different.

For the time being, however, the reality of the jukebox meant a motley array of machines, ranging from the latest *Singing Tower* and *Victory* to decrepit pre-light-up models, for entertaining Americans at home and abroad. Nonetheless wired music systems grew in popularity, partly because they could fall back on a library of music to supplement the shortage of discs, and partly because of the human element. For instance, in 1943 the *Los Angeles Times* reported that 18 female disc jockeys of the Wilshire Amusement Company (described as the 'World's largest juke mill') 'Say that the telephonic small talk that results when a nickel clinks into the juke boxes is often "Out of Saroyan". Lonely soldiers on shore leave sometimes deposit ten or fifteen dollars an evening in a jukebox just to have someone to talk with".' The same article gave a glimpse of a

futuristic post-war world in which there would be television jukeboxes 'which will produce an alluring voice, music, plus a movie of the juke girl,' adding 'the girls are finding it difficult enough now to avoid the jukebox dates, to say nothing of proposals.'

Romance was not the only extracurricular activity for the wired systems. It was reported that they were used to rouse sailors from bars when an emergency called for shore leave to be immediately cancelled. A further novel use was revealed when Detroit newspapers of 1942 reported a court case under the heading 'Telephone Music used as a front for Bookies', which involved the illegal supply of racing information. 'One of the offices used in the set-up was equipped with what is known in the trade as a telephone music outfit. Police said it was a front for the outfit to give racing information to bookies . . .'

By the beginning of 1945 there was a different kind of speculation in the trade press. With increasing competition between a growing band of jukebox manufacturers, it was uncertain how many would remain profitable and survive. The prevailing opinion was that not only would there be revolutionary new machines from the traditional producers, including AMI, John Gable, Mills Industries, Packard, Rock-ola, Seebury, and Wurlitzer but a likely influx of industrial giants (RCA, Philco, Westinghouse, Zenith, Emerson & Farnsworth) keen to exploit the market. Although there seemed to be innumerable potential applications of the new technology to jukeboxes, which had hitherto been characterised by a quest for mechanical reliability and stunning styling rather than great sophistication, only four of the established manufacturers survived into the next decade and beyond. Gable, Mills and Packard all perished in the post-war turmoil, and all the while newcomers came and went.

Chapter Four
Now you hear it . . .
now you don't

The immediate euphoria and relief that came with the
end of hostilities was short lived. For many, picking up the
threads of normal life was traumatic, while industry found,
to quote the catchphrase of the time, 'it couldn't turn swords into
ploughshares overnight.' And in the meantime the communities
which had sprung up around, and geared themselves exclusively to
industrial, military, and naval centres dispersed, while life ebbed
from the bars and clubs which had been the focal point of
wartime leisure.

The music industry was surprised to discover that as family life was resumed the jukebox was in danger of losing the special place it had acquired in the war years. To make matters worse, there were no new exciting designs to stimulate interest, and the jukebox that had been a good friend through the war suddenly looked like a tired old relic from an era most people were keen to put behind them. The continuing shortage of materials and labour (with many ex-servicemen taking time off before returning to work, or taking advantage of new educational courses), industrial unrest and the winding down of existing government contracts meant that only AMI could offer 'new' machines in 1945. In reality they belonged to the venerable *Singing Towers*. In addition to the existing *201*s and factory-rebuilt versions, the mechanism was guaranteed as new and housed in a redesigned cabinet. Although still called *Singing Towers* they were given a new model number – *301*.

At the same time Wurlitzer was advertising the *Victory*, described as 'the only new model since Pearl Harbour'. But in general jukebox companies, like the rest of manufacturing industry, was relying on tantalising adverts assuring customers that patience would be rewarded by outstanding new models in the near future. In the meantime, rumours abounded. Would the jukebox itself be threatened by new technological developments?

In fact the changes that did occur on the music scene went as follows. Tradio Inc, the main manufacturer of coin-operated radios (abundantly available), was about to launch coin-operated television, and several companies were now bringing out coin-operated loudspeakers (which had first appeared in 1939, but with the 1942 introduction of a timer could now be used to supply a given amount of background music. Seeburg had yet to bring out its background music system, but others were working on the idea, and there were systems such as the *John-Lee* marketed by Musical Minutes Inc, whereby a pair of linked 16-selector Wurlitzer mechanisms could offer a programme of two hours of continuous music before repeating. Meanwhile newcomers to the field threw their hats into the ring, including Bally, the pinball giants, who announced it would apply its electronic expertise to the John Gable mechanism. The trade press of the time reported this 'race' as follows:

Nine starters are in the '1946 Phono Derby' –
Aireon, AMI, Bally, Gable, Mills, Packard, Rock-ola,
Seeburg and Wurlitzer. Capehart will divide his
time between Washington and Indianapolis and
enter the field with his own machine. Add three
new Dark Horses. Roberts has left Mills and is
reported to be linking up with Kressburg, formerly
of Seeburg, on a deal with Filben to manufacture a
phonograph. Majestic is rumoured to still be on
the prowl and interested in this field and Zenith is
considering a coin-operated mechanism. This
would make an even dozen contenders for operator
business in '46. Hold onto your hats boys!'

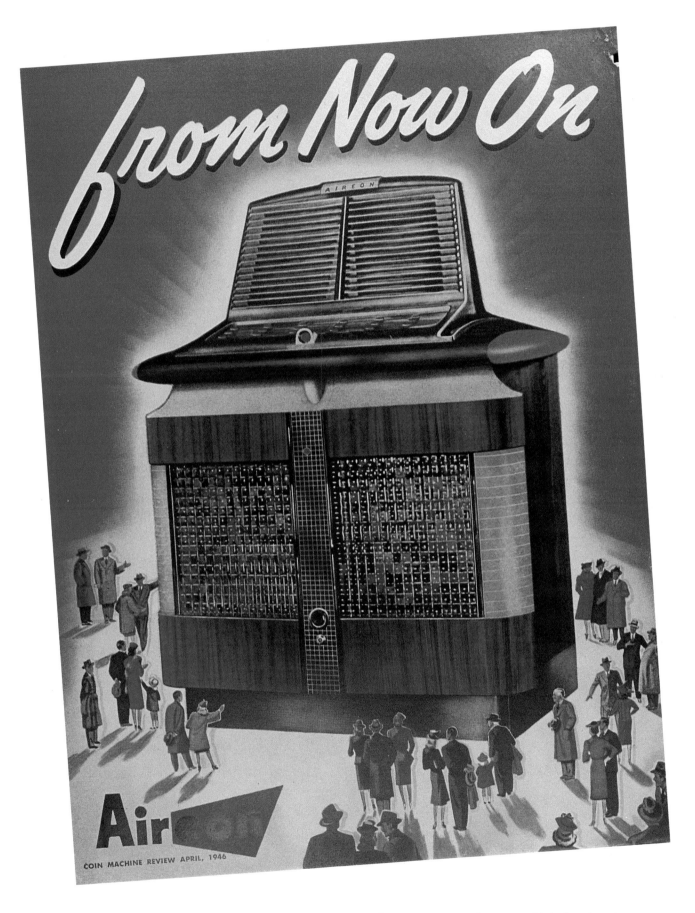

COIN MACHINE REVIEW APRIL, 1946

The newcomer Aireon beat its established rivals in the race to bring out the first post-war jukebox, backed with an extensive advertising campaign.

Although auxiliary speakers were not new, Seeburg promoted them in conjunction with the **Trashcan** as 'scientific sound distribution'.

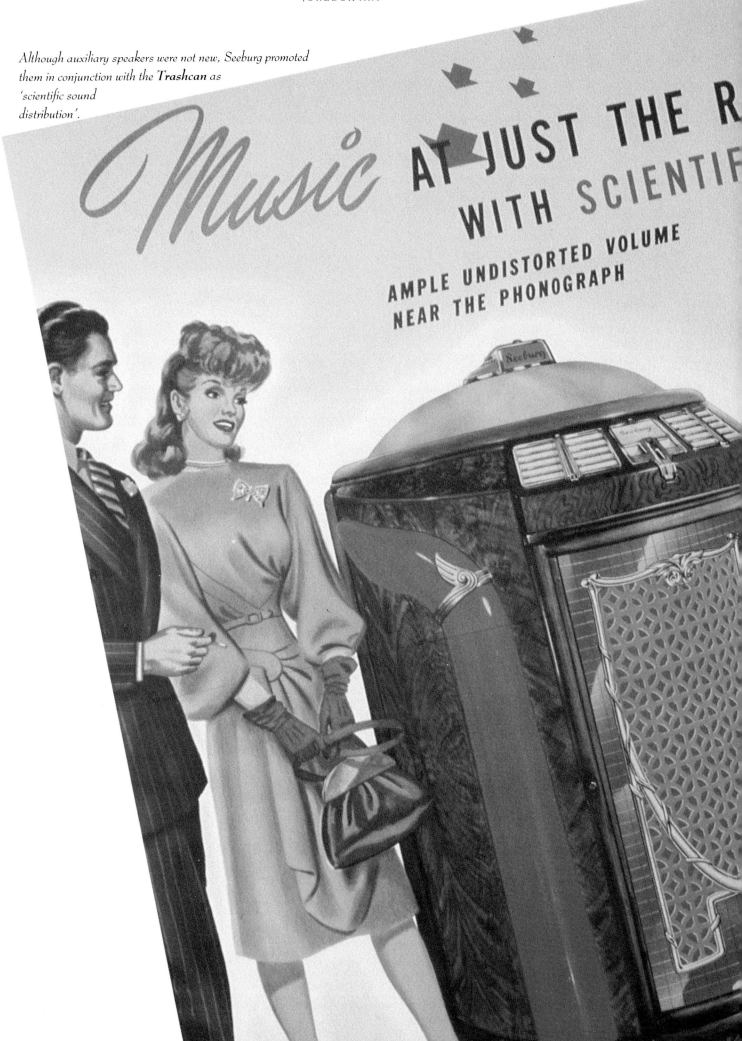

Music AT JUST THE R
WITH SCIENTIF

AMPLE UNDISTORTED VOLUME
NEAR THE PHONOGRAPH

HT LEVEL FOR EVERYBODY!
SOUND DISTRIBUTION

...A coin slips into the single chute.

...A finger touches a favorite selection.

...Silently, without clatter, the record slides into place below the featherweight pickup.

The public is not conscious of the mechanism... conscious only of the brilliant tones of the music being played...all the subtle harmonies of the recording artist faithfully reproduced.

Those near the phonograph listen to the music with pleasure...there is no distortion...no blare.

Those in quiet booths far from the phonograph do not need to strain their ears to catch the words of their favorite song. Softly, at conversational level, the music comes to them...providing a rich background for their relaxing moments of pleasure.

Listening to music provided by Scientific Sound Distribution is a happy experience...an experience only possible with a Seeburg Music System.

MUSIC AT CONVERSATIONAL LEVEL THROUGHOUT THE LOCATION

SCIENTIFIC SOUND DISTRIBUTION

Seeburg

1902 • DEPENDABLE MUSIC SYSTEMS • 1947

YOUR SEEBURG DISTRIBUTOR FOR A DEMONSTRATION

Stop— Linger and Listen!

Musical Fun for Everyone

Want to add fun to your trip? Take this tip. Pause here and there where you can enjoy Wurlitzer Music. It's guaranteed to add joy to your journey.

Each friendly oasis invites you to stop for a snack, to linger and listen to your favorite tunes played by the world's top bands as only a Wurlitzer can play them. The Rudolph Wurlitzer Company, North Tonawanda, New York. ★ ★ ★ See Phonograph Section of Classified Telephone Directory for names of Wurlitzer Dealers.

The *Sign of the Musical Note* identifies places where you can have fun playing a Wurlitzer.

WURLiTzer
PHONOGRAPH
Music

THE NAME THAT MEANS *Music* TO MILLION

The music of Wurlitzer pianos, accordions commercial phonographs and electronic organs is heard "'round the world." The Rudolph Wurlitzer Company is America's largest manufacturer of pianos all sold under one name...also the nation's largest, best known producer of juke boxes and accordions

"Having a wonderful time"

ALBERT DORNE

Musical Fun for Everyone

Nothing will spur vacationists to send the home folks glowing reports of the wonderful time they are having like the fun at resorts where there is Wurlitzer Music.

For there's nothing like the latest hits by top bands to foster good fellowship, good times and a grand vacation.

Whether you head for the mountains, the lakes or the seashore, look for the place that has Wurlitzer Music and you'll find fun. The Rudolph Wurlitzer Company, North Tonawanda, New York. ★★★ See Phonograph Section of Classified Telephone Directory for names of Wurlitzer Dealers.

The *Sign of the Musical Note* identifies places where you can have fun playing a Wurlitzer.

WURLITZER PHONOGRAPH MUSIC

THE NAME THAT MEANS *Music* TO MILLIONS

The music of Wurlitzer pianos, accordions, commercial phonographs and electronic organs is heard "'round the world." The Rudolph Wurlitzer Company is America's largest manufacturer of pianos all sold under one name...also the nation's largest, best known producer of juke boxes and accordions.

The Waltz She Will Always Remember

Musical Fun for Everyone

Celebrating a marriage, an anniversary or some other highlight in your life? Make it a party you'll always remember.

Go where they have a Wurlitzer. Music by the best entertainers and bands in the land will add a gay and tuneful touch to the occasion.

Long after the party is over, the Wurlitzer melodies that brightened those fun-filled moments will linger to stir priceless memories of the time, the place and the friends who helped you celebrate. The Rudolph Wurlitzer Company, North Tonawanda, N.Y. ★★★ See Phonograph Section of Classified Telephone Directory for names of Wurlitzer Dealers.

The *Sign of the Musical Note* identifies places where you can have fun playing a Wurlitzer.

THE NAME THAT MEANS *Music* **TO MILLIONS**

The music of Wurlitzer pianos, accordions, commercial phonographs and electronic organs is heard "'round the world." The Rudolph Wurlitzer Company is America's largest manufacturer of pianos all sold under one name...also the nation's largest, best known producer of juke boxes and accordions.

The Magic That Changes Moods!

Musical Fun for Everyone

The old saying, "Two's company, three's a crowd," doesn't always hold. There are times when every couple longs for music, laughter and the companionship of a crowd.

Whenever you long for such diversion, you will find it wherever there is Wurlitzer Music. Before you hang up your hat, you will be having fun.

Like magic, you will find Wurlitzer Music will change your mood, brighten and lighten your outlook. You will go home refreshed and relaxed for having had a wonderful time. The Rudolph Wurlitzer Company, North Tonawanda, N. Y. ★★★ See Phonograph Section of Classified Telephone Directory for names of Wurlitzer Dealers.

The Sign of the Musical Note identifies places where you can have fun playing a Wurlitzer.

WURLITZER
PHONOGRAPH
MUSIC

THE NAME THAT MEANS *Music* TO MILLIONS
The music of Wurlitzer pianos, accordions and commercial phonographs is heard "round the world." Wurlitzer, America's largest manufacturer of pianos all produced under one name ... also America's largest, best-known manufacturer of juke boxes and accordions, now has in production a great new electronic organ.

After the Easter Parade...

Musical Fun for Everyone

Bright Easter finery. A smart Easter hat. Gay Easter flowers. It's every woman's right to glow with pride in the Easter parade. And, it's no woman's wish to go home and spend the rest of the day in the kitchen.

There's a hint for husbands here. Take the family out for dinner—where they have Wurlitzer Music. Your friends will be there with their families. All of you, young and old, will have fun talking, laughing and listening to tunes as stimulating as your first fresh breath of spring. The Rudolph Wurlitzer Company, North Tonawanda, New York. ★ ★ ★ See Phonograph Section of Classified Telephone Directory for names of Wurlitzer Dealers.

The *Sign of the Musical Note* identifies places where you can have fun playing a Wurlitzer.

THE NAME THAT MEANS *Music* **TO MILLIONS**
The music of Wurlitzer pianos, accordions, commercial phonographs and electronic organs is heard "round the world." The Rudolph Wurlitzer Company is America's largest manufacturer of pianos all sold under one name...also the nation's largest, best known producer of juke boxes and accordions.

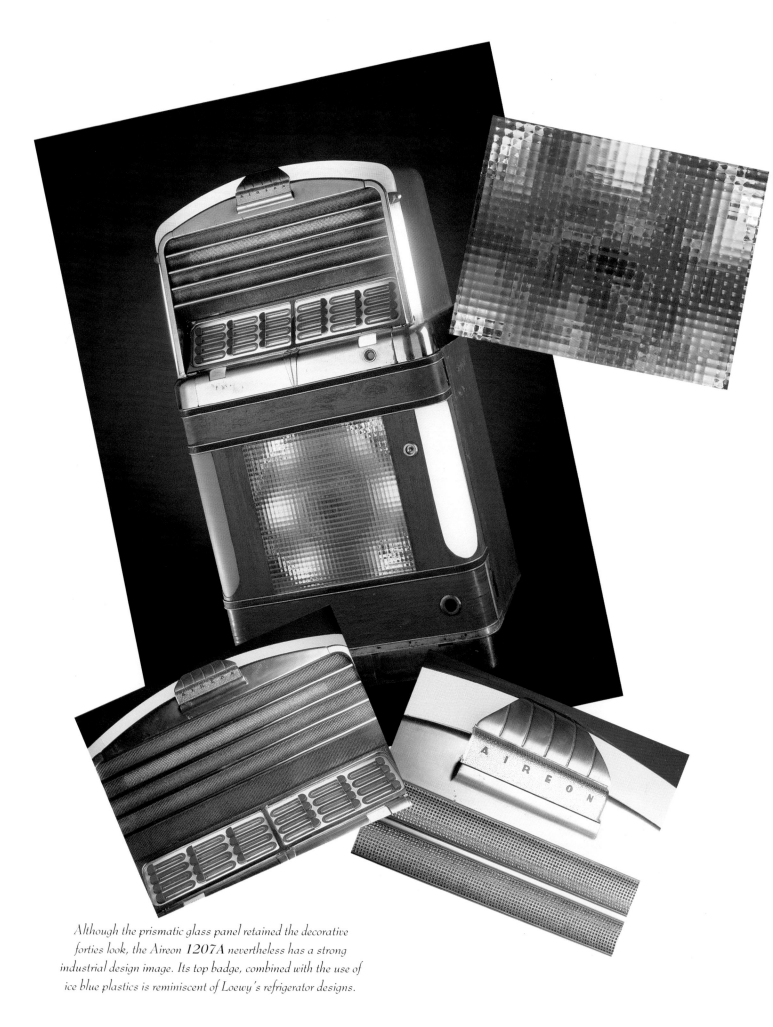

Although the prismatic glass panel retained the decorative
forties look, the Aireon 1207A nevertheless has a strong
industrial design image. Its top badge, combined with the use of
ice blue plastics is reminiscent of Loewy's refrigerator designs.

jukebox to one dime. The controversy spilled over into 1947, when the *New York Daily News* featured a cartoon of a jukebox with outstretched arms, captioned 'Brother can you spare a dime.' Wurlitzer consequently dropped their slogan.

The main rival to the Wurlitzer *1015* was Seeburg's new jukebox, the *P 146*, whose distinctive opening lid and semi-cylindrical shape had earned it the nickname 'the Trashcan'. As innovative in style as the *Aireon*, it had the advantage of the reliable pre-war mechanism as well as Seeburg's good reputation. Seeburg emphasised its 'scien-

tific' sound, expanding on the pre-war concept of the jukebox now linked to extension speakers, otherwise known as the teardrop and the bigger and more ornate mirror (now often called the

The Wurlitzer 1080 was advertised in the same manner as the 1015, driving home the message that Wurlitzer was 'the name that means Music to millions'.

roadhouse). With the advantage of hindsight we now know the 'Trashcan' series (1946–48) was a stop-gap measure. Nevertheless it remains a classic design which together with Aireon, Filben and Mills exemplifies 1940s industrial design aesthetics.

Meanwhile in 1946 Rock-ola shared Wurlitzer's faith in mainstream, bright, colourful jukebox art. Like Seeburg, the essential design of their machine, the Model 1422 was carried on into two further models although the last of the series, the 1428, brought out in 1948, featured less metal, relying on elaborately moulded plastic for its visual

impact. AMI also favoured the decorative look, the 1946 Model A turning its back on the art-deco skyscraper image which had made the *Singing Towers* so distinctive, instead opting for elaborate, garishly lit, sculpted, opaque plastic. In addition,

Remaining essentially the same through three model changes, the 1946–1948 Trashcan was one of the most successful late forties jukeboxes.

119

Fun for the Crowd but Hard Work for the Juke Box

Nickel after nickel, hour after hour, the music goes round and round. It's grand fun for the boys and girls, but tough on the phonograph instrument.

To stand such hard playing night after night, juke boxes have to be sturdily built. Stamina is a "must" for internal parts—especially for capacitors, which have so much to do with the tone quality and smoothness of the music. That's why, in increasing thousands of juke boxes, Mallory FP (Fabricated Plate) Capacitors are standard equipment.

Mallory FP Capacitors are designed to give service far beyond the ordinary. They are built with the knowledge of long experience—experience proving that when a capacitor is safeguarded against internal corrosion, its operating life is enormously extended. They are manufactured with extreme care and processing control.

For instance, hospital gauze is not pure enough to be used in the anodes of these Mallory capacitors. Mallory employees are required to wear rubber gloves so that body salts, which play havoc with capacitor life, cannot enter the cartridges. These are details, only two of many, that explain why the impurity level of Mallory FP Capacitors is held to the incredible level of *less than one-half part per million.*

It takes a sturdy phonograph to play hour after hour—and that's where Mallory Capacitors come in

This capacity for precise manufacturing control is a hallmark of Mallory in all its products—capacitors, contacts, rectifiers, resistors, switches, vibrators, resistance welding electrodes. It is backed by thirty years of engineering experience that have made these products the standards of industry everywhere.

If you have a problem within our scope

sic World are on ROCK-OLA
- Sioux City.

the distinction of being "The
. . . leading the industry as
sective, coin operated music

enced Route Operator new
ence and matchless economy.
cation owner new heights of
manship . . . to hold and

Do it more successfully, more
with ROCK-OLA Equipment.

Above Although basically the same as the 1946 model *1424*,
Rock-ola's *1426* of the next year showed that full peacetime
production had returned by the extensive use of metal castings
rather than the previous model's wooden grille *(right)*.

AMI increased its number of selections, unlike Rock-ola, Seeburg and Wurlitzer, who had retained their existing mechanical set-up. One school of thought argued that the jukebox should only be stocked with current favourites, all of which would be played intensively, but AMI decided the future lay in offering a greater choice. The *Model* A therefore had a mechanism offering 40 selections. Defending this expansion AMI issued the following statement:

Music has played an important part in American life and acted as a tonic even in the most difficult time. Phonographs won't stop playing when our music loving Americans get out to enjoy the new automatic phones and the new records, for now the war is over a market that has been starved during the past several years will have to be satisfied. The popularity of the phonograph has increased and it is the best source of music, variety and selection. The automatic phonograph throbs with life when the nickel impulse sets the platter spinning. Selectivity emphasises the appeal of automatic music and feeds the customer's hunger for certain tunes. With increased selectivity, interest jumps to a higher level. The very variety of abundant selection is bound to spice up the location and stimulate player appeal. We feel increased selectivity is a rich plum for both operator and location owner.

*Even the economy **Pla-Mor** (below) had an air of luxury, while the massive motorised ballroom speaker **(right)** added glamour to a hidden installation.*

HOMER E. CAPEHART'S
PACKARD PLA-MOR
Model 7
for 1947

Your Phonograph

Rich walnut with a softly glowing lighted plastic crown—
Highlights and shadows that glow and gleam—
Romantic and appealing—as captivating as firelight—
Gay—but not garish—
Beautiful—but not bizarre
As entrancing as a rainbow—

HOMER E. CAPEHART'S
PACKARD PLA-MOR
Speaker 1000
"OUT-OF-THIS-WORLD"

Breath-taking

Homer E. Capehart's
Packard Pla-Mor Phono-
graph Hideaway
Model 400
The smoothest, simplest,
most desirable hide-
away phonograph in
Automatic Music History

Scintillating—Sparkling—Effervescent—

Exciting as rare champagne—

Perfect for the Dream-Boats and Wonder-Bars—

Fills the room with dancing bubbles of light—

Operates with the Packard Pla-Mor Phonograph

Hideaway (Shown at left)—With the beautiful

Packard Model 7—or any phonograph.

Meanwhile, other manufacturers were mooting the idea of mega-selections. Reports were heard of a Swedish invention (also of 1947) which was a 'revolutionary new automatic phonograph which virtually provides a complete music library on tap. This consisted of a record stack holding 50 discs providing about 7 hours of continuous music. The records are held in an upright position and are played in the same position. Records do not turn over. Two turntables revolving in opposite directions are provided for playing both sides of a disc, and two tone arms are employed . . .' It was thought that this system, with a radio, could become a home entertainment unit or a jukebox, but there is no evidence that this idea was greeted with any excitement. The trade was used to hearing stories of brilliant inventions, and multi-selection was still not regarded as particularly desirable. Future developments were eventually confirmed by Seeburg. At the end of the decade it brought out a 100-selection machine that settled the question once and for all.

The new wave of small post-war manufacturers were unfettered by any established image, leaving them free to bring out adventurous new designs.

Prestige **AND PROFIT**

ARE YOURS WITH...

THE "*Manhattan*"

CREATED BY HOMER E. CAPEHART

Prestige ... Distinctive! New as tomorrow! Utterly different from any other phonograph—the magnificent Manhattan *graces* any location. Inspired styling, superb tone and ready-for-anything dependability command admiration and approval from music patrons, location owners and music operators—everywhere! The Manhattan is a blueblood! Born to the manor! Equally at home in the moderne bar of chrome, brilliance and flash! Or the reserved club of quiet dignity and subdued colors. Wherever it is installed, Manhattan *prestige* creates customer goodwill and sells music!

PROFIT ... Preferred product! Direct-to-Ops sales plan! Only Packard gives you both, *Mr. Operator.* By ordering direct from the factory you receive the $1010 Manhattan phonograph for $625.50 cash, or $100 down and $24.43 per month for 25 months and $24.41 for one month. That's why Packard, more than any other music manufacturer, offers you *business opportunity.* Opportunity to make more money! Opportunity to replace worn-out equipment! Opportunity to establish your business and future, securely! Music Ops hail Packard's new direct sales plan as—*only deal today for an operator.* To profit from it, *you must act!* Mail coupon at right for complete information. Today! Now!

Only Deal Today For An Oper...
... Say Music Ops from C...

I am a bona fide Operator of...
in ....

Please send me full ...
sales plan, your ...
tell me ex...
Packard ...

SEE CURRENT
PRICE LIST
REVERSE
SIDE

NEW
LOW
PRICES

PACKARD
Continues to Offer
The MUSIC MERCHANTS
of AMERICA The

Finest
Wall Box
PLA-MOR 5 Cent HI-CHROME

BY FAR THE MOST PROFITABLE—
COST AGAINST INTAKE

• NEVER WEARS OUT
• NEVER OBSOLETE
• TROUBLE FREE

INDIANAPOLIS INDIANA

PACKARD MANUFACTURING CORP. • NOBLE AT MARKET ST. •

Packhard's novel selection system was by means of a wallbox incorporated into the cabinets of the **Pla-mor** *and* **Manhattan**. *Known as the Butler, this on its own became a universal selector, much used with other manufacturers' equipment.*

71

The post-war jukebox scene was still in a state of flux. Challenge Industries announced a 30-selection machine, but within a few months the company was under congressional investigation and during this time one of its factories burnt down in suspicious circumstances. Concerned as ever about a bad press, the jukebox establishment was horrifed at the scandal: 'Wait until it is revealed that the firm is now in the newspaper-classed Coin Machine Business. The fireworks will start immediately'. One good outcome was that the 30-selection mechanism was taken over by Filben, producers of one of the most visually distinctive jukeboxes of all time.

By 1947 the worst of America's production problems were resolved, but the nation was now facing economic problems raising the spectre of recession. However, the jukebox industry eventually settled down to a balance of power which was much the same as in 1942. And to complete the picture Senator Homer Capehart returned to the fray with the Packard Corporation's *Pla-mor* jukebox. Although this is a distinctive piece of equipment, Packard is best remembered for the wall box which accompanied the *Pla-mor* jukebox. Its adaptability ensured its survival long after the *Pla-mor* had gone. In 1948 Packard brought out its last model, the luxurious *Manhattan*. The demise of Packard, and the departure of Capehart from the scene, meant a major strand of jukebox history was at an end. Meanwhile Mills was desperately trying to keep its name alive by advertising the exciting prospect of a new jukebox. In fact post-war production was proving especially difficult for the company. If anything, Mills was by now more associated with the Panoram than the jukebox, so it could not even count on extensive customer loyalty. A further problem was the rush to buy other manufacturer's new equipment in 1946; this, coupled with a downturn in the nation's economy, put Mills, as latecomers, at a disadvantage. Mills Industries other divisions were back in production with refrigeration, a sophisticated dispenser for Coca-Cola which, unlike the existing bottle vendors, actually mixed the drink and was capable of vending 180 cups of fresh coke an hour, and the development of the Panoram into Sono-Vision, a marketing and educational audio-visual aid.

The Mills' phonograph division was at this time burdened with the development costs of a new 40-selection mechanism, and an obsession with quality that resulted in the 1947 *Constellation* being the most over-engineered jukebox of all time. However, the design of the *Constellation* had the distinction of being one of only a handful to step outside the parameters of jukebox aesthetics into the wider area of American industrial design. Like Seeburgs 1948 *Model 148* 'Trashcan' the cabinet was all-aluminium, but whereas the Seeburg was simply an existing design transferred from wood into metal, with the metal finished in artificial wood grain, the Mills was very special. The seamless cabinet made by the Bell Aircraft Corporation had an immaculate painted finish, (in blue, burgundy or gold) and relied on an understated decorative aluminium grill and moving coloured light to provide the mandatory visual entertainment. Yet in spite of all this the *Constellation*, together with the de-luxe version the *Ensemble*, (which was matched to a stylish extension speaker) hardly stood a chance. Not only had production delays made them latecomers, but the new mechanism gave teething troubles, and these, as with Aireon, became a jinx. Other divisions of Mills were also having problems, and this historic company, one of America's oldest, suffered the ignominy of chapter 11 (voluntary) bankruptcy in 1949. Despite the hype and undoubted success of the Wurlitzer *1015*, the jukebox market was not the gold mine many had predicted it would be. The departure of Mills spelt out there was no room for mistakes. The *Constellation* suffered one final indignity – being taken over by Evans.

In 1946 Wurlitzer determined to return to the heady days of the early 1940s. The *1015* was soon joined by the radically different *Model 1080 Colonial*, a serpentine eighteenth century-style cabinet enhanced with discreetly lit mirror panels which contrasted drastically with the *1015*. However, it was advertised in the same manner, in popular magazines, offered as a relatively conservative jukebox suitable for establishments which would otherwise find the idea unacceptable. In fact this marketing route had already been taken with the *780*, and was further proof that Wurlitzer had one foot in the past. In contrast they advertised the

Right In contrast with the general move towards a new, modern style, Wurlitzer's 1080 was an exercise in nostalgia. Its eighteenth century-styled cabinet was designed to appeal to conservative sites where a conventional jukebox would look out of place.

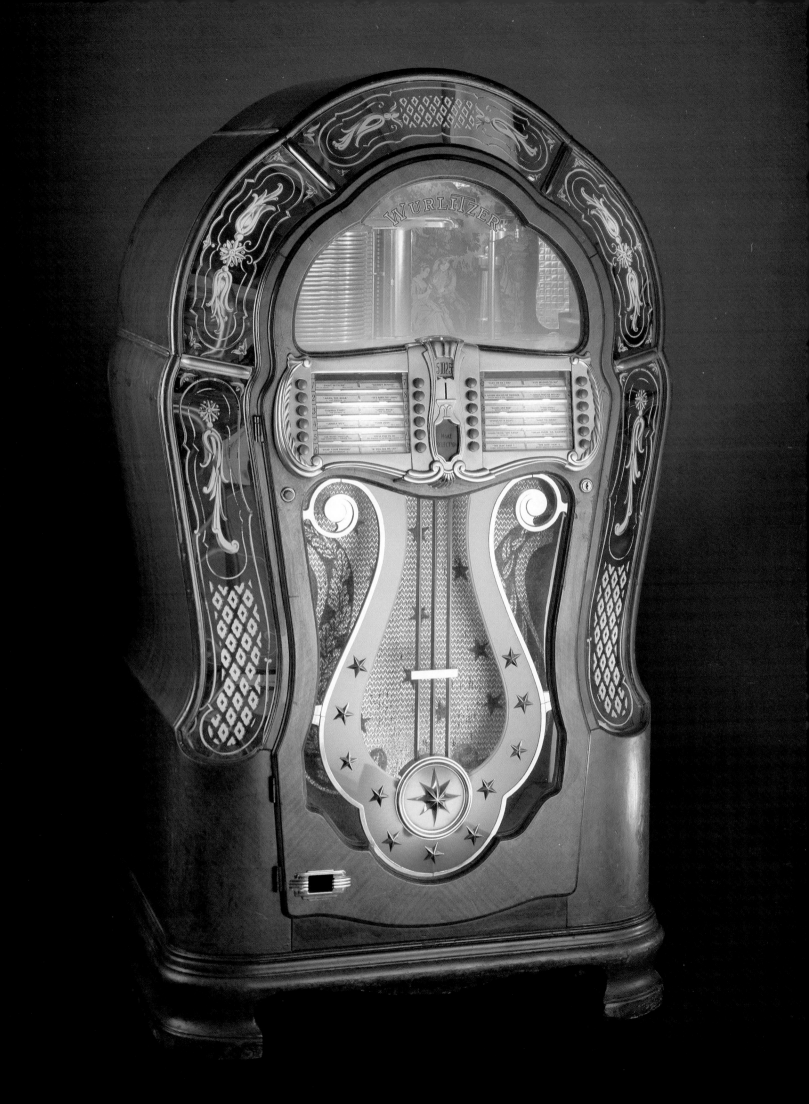

Above and Right *Every detail of the 1080 emphasised its*
antique look, with even the back door mural evoking eighteenth
century luxury.

1947 Model 1100 as the first real post-war jukebox. Destined to be the last designed by Paul Fuller, who thereafter retired through ill-health, it is in many ways the last real Wurlitzer. From this point on the company's once special image dwindled in the eyes of the public. Design rather than technology had always been the main ingredient of its success, only in the post-war period design made few concessions to the future.

The main features of the 1100 included a reduced scale (1945 trade press predictions were for smaller, lightweight designs), pared down and simplified decorative metal work, a wood-grain one-piece aluminium 'front-door', a massive 'bomber window' dome which opened up revealing the

Right The last jukebox designed by Paul Fuller retained the glamour which had made Wurlitzer so distinctive, whilst recognising the trend towards smaller, lighter machines.

Below Brilliant, faceted plastics gave a harder quality to the moving coloured light that had been one of Fuller's trademarks.

Always the Life of the Party

Musical Fun for Everyone

Start the New Year right by having fun! Get your group together. Head for a place that has Wurlitzer Music. Along with you goes a tuneful guarantee of a grand and glorious time.

Nothing like these gay music makers to prove the life of the party. Hit tunes. Top entertainers. Laughter and fun galore.

You'll leave with a new resolution . . . a promise to spend more fun-filled hours in '48 where they have Wurlitzer Music. The Rudolph Wurlitzer Company, North Tonawanda, N. Y. ★★★ See Phonograph Section of Classified Telephone Directory for names of Wurlitzer Music Merchants.

The Sign of the Musical Note identifies places where you can have fun playing a Wurlitzer.

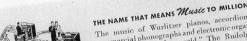

THE NAME THAT MEANS *Music* **TO MILLIONS**
The music of Wurlitzer pianos, accordions, commercial phonographs and electronic organs is heard "'round the world." The Rudolph Wurlitzer Company is America's largest manufacturer of pianos all sold under one name . . . also the nation's largest, best known producer of juke boxes and accordions.

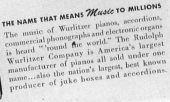

Above and *Overleaf* There was some truth in the claim that Wurlitzer was 'the name that means music to millions'.

Go where you can play
this Brilliant NEW WURLiTZER!

Zenith COBRA TONE ARM

Next time you are out for fun and refreshments, go where you can play this brilliant new Wurlitzer Model 1100. Never before have you seen or heard a coin-operated phonograph with so many fun-producing features. Light, color, action! Sensational, moving, ever-changing illumination. Majestic tone that can be regulated to the sound level most pleasing to your taste. There's more *Musical Fun for Everyone* wherever there's one of these colorful, tuneful new Wurlitzers!

WATCH IT IN ACTION

Its panoramic Sky-Top turret window gives you a ringside seat. See the records change and watch Zenith's Cobra Tone Arm play them. This sensational new tone arm eliminates record surface noise—enhances Wurlitzer's famous tone. The music sounds as though the entertainers were right in the room with you.

NEW *Encore* PROGRAM SELECTOR ...is faster, easier—more fun. It rotates 24 popular record titles into view in 3 easy-to-see programs of 8 great tunes each.

Musical Fun for Everyone

The Sign of the Musical Note *identifies places where you ca have fun playing a Wurlitzer.*

HOW YOU CAN SEE AND PLAY THIS NEV WURLITZER—*If you would like to see and play this ne Wurlitzer in your favorite place for food and refreshment tell the proprietor to get in touch with his nearest Wurlitze Music Merchant, or tear out the coupon and ask him to sen it to us. We will tell him how he can obtain one of these ne Wurlitzers for your entertainment. The Rudolph Wurlitze Company, North Tonawanda, New York.* ★★★ *See Phone graph Section of Classified Telephone Directory for names c Wurlitzer Music Merchants.*

THE RUDOLPH WURLITZER COMPANY
Dept. LA, North Tonawanda, New York

Please tell me how I can provide a new Model 1100 Wurlitzer for the entertainment of my customers.

FIRM NAME

ADDRESS

CITY   STATE   ZONE

On Main Street—
Highways and Byways

Musical Fun for Everyone

Go where you will. Look and listen as you go. Everywhere people are having fun to Wurlitzer Music.

That's the kind of music it is. Catchy tunes that start you singing. Lively tunes that stimulate fellowship and fun. Popular tunes, the music *of* the people, *by* the top entertainers, *for* your enjoyment.

Next time you go out for food or refreshment, go in where they have Wurlitzer Music. You'll find that good tunes and good times always go together. The Rudolph Wurlitzer Company, North Tonawanda, New York. ★ ★ ★ See Phonograph Section of Classified Telephone Directory for names of Wurlitzer Dealers.

The *Sign of the Musical Note* identifies places where you can have fun playing a Wurlitzer.

WURLITZER PHONOGRAPH MUSIC

THE NAME THAT MEANS *Music* **TO MILLIONS**
The music of Wurlitzer pianos, accordions, commercial phonographs and electronic organs is heard "'round the world." The Rudolph Wurlitzer Company is America's largest manufacturer of pianos all sold under one name...also the nation's largest, best known producer of juke boxes and accordions.

There's a Witchery to WURLITZER MUSIC

Musical Fun for Everyone

Call it magic, witchery or what you will...Wurlitzer Music has a way of making any occasion a bigger occasion. More fun. More life. More laughter. Remember it the next time you're out for entertainment. Go where they have Wurlitzer Music. Sweet or swing, vibrant or mellow, the musical pulse of America is at your fingertips. The Rudolph Wurlitzer Company, North Tonawanda, New York. ★ ★ ★ See Phonograph Section of Classified Telephone Directory for names of Wurlitzer Dealers.

The Sign of the Musical Note identifies places where you can have fun playing a Wurlitzer. ➤

WURLITZER PHONOGRAPH MUSIC

THE NAME THAT MEANS *Music* **TO MILLIONS**
The music of Wurlitzer pianos, accordions, commercial phonographs and electronic organs is heard "round the world." The Rudolph Wurlitzer Company is America's largest manufacturer of pianos all sold under one name...also the nation's largest, best known producer of juke boxes and accordions.

Above The 1100 was the last machine to feature in Wurlitzer's post-war marketing campaign. The jukebox was now under threat from television and background music, losing the public appeal which Wurlitzer had striven to achieve.

81

changer mechanism, and faceted clear lower plastics which had the effect of producing a brilliant, hard light from the revolving colour cylinders which represented a final link with pre-war style. Although the changer system remained essentially the same with no indication that Wurlitzer thought the public may be getting bored with it or that it envisaged increasing the 24-selection, the sound and selection systems were radical improvements. The *1100* was now equipped with the new, lightweight, plastic Zenith tone arm, with a crystal cartridge and a 'floating' stylus. This system necessitated the introduction of a pre-amp and although not the first use of crystal cartridges which Rockola had pioneered, the slender Cobra tone arm gave visual emphasis to a more delicate and sensitive handling of records. The *1100* also featured an animated electric title display which served to provoke interest in the titles because a button had to be pressed to view the entire selection. This also did away with the array of buttons which had been a feature of previous models,

achieving a neat, compact look. The new sound system was incorporated into those *1080*s which had remained unsold, and the 'new' model was designated the *1080 A*.

Another company to realise small meant beautiful, now that jukeboxes were no longer the social phenomenon they had once been, was AMI. Its scaled down Model B of 1948 retained elaborate moulded plastic, though now confined to the top canopy. It was available in a choice of either light or dark finished wooden cabinets. Such changes however, could do little to counter the threat from a revolutionary form of entertainment – the television.

By 1948 the jukebox was under threat from new competition. Television was not only keeping people at home but also appearing in bars, where the jukebox had once reigned. The New York Television Company now introduced a system linking the TV with personalised speakers, a nickel allowing the patron six minutes of television listening. To add insult to injury, the Telejuke Corporation introduced the *Speedway*, a television unit designed to be mounted on a jukebox, as well as a special cabinet to house both a jukebox and television. With the government announcing the opening up of wave bands to allow a projected 900 TV stations, this was a real threat.

*Left The AMI **Model B** fell in with the general trend towards smaller jukeboxes, and although the top canopy was of ornately moulded plastic, the design demonstrates the move away from ostentatious styling.*

Right Alternatives to the Jukebox – sophisticated music systems which would make the colourful, coin-operated machines obsolete – now threatened the industry.

Even as a source of music, the jukebox was vulnerable. In the home some 66 million radio sets received broadcasts from about 2,000 radio stations, and the growth in domestic record players looked set to match that figure. Meanwhile, out of the home background music was becoming commonplace, with companies such as the Storecast Corporation providing this service for grocery stores. As more Americans stayed at home bars, clubs and restaurants reported a downturn in trade, and were increasingly using TV or background music (either coin-operated or free) rather

than the jukebox. Contemporary trade reports questioned whether there were now as many jukeboxes as in the pre-war days, while a finance house confirmed that the average operator was buying 1 or 2 jukeboxes at a time in contrast with 5 or 10 in

Far right The 1958 Rock-ola *1458* (120 selections) together with its companion model, the two hundred selection model *1465*, represent the last of the fifties 'bandshell' look. Both were also assembled in Europe, differing from the American originals only in cabinet finish.

Below and right AMI's *Automatic Hostess* continued the pre-war idea of the telephone jukebox, whereby girl 'dee jays' operating from a 'juke mill' offered a selection from a music library.

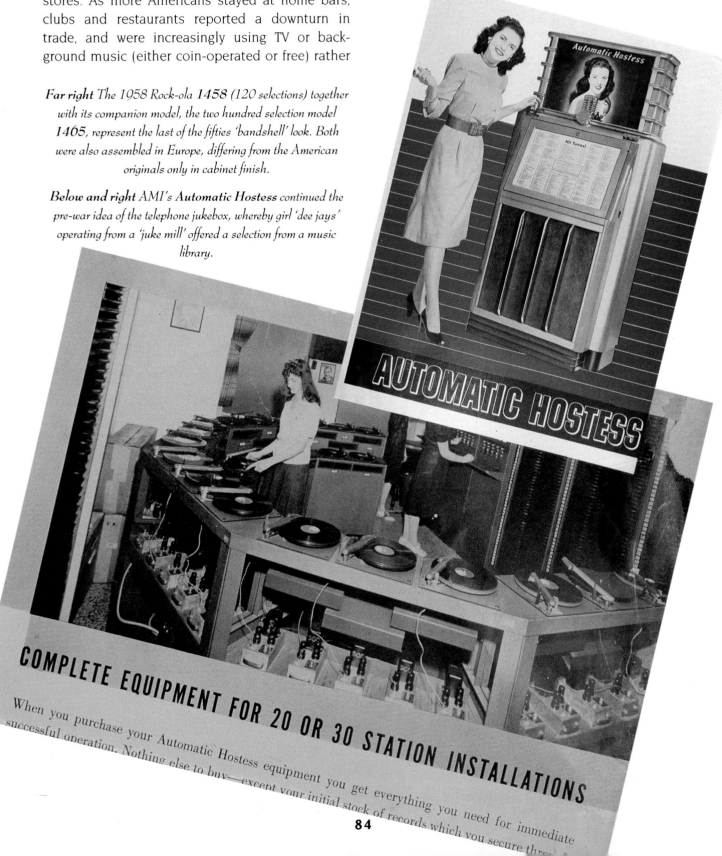

AUTOMATIC HOSTESS

COMPLETE EQUIPMENT FOR 20 OR 30 STATION INSTALLATIONS

When you purchase your Automatic Hostess equipment you get everything you need for immediate successful operation. Nothing else to buy—except your initial stock of records which you secure thr...

1940. Jukebox operators were told that background music was not a threat.

Heaven is supposed to be a place of eternal music, so it is not likely that people will become surfeited on music – good music. It does mean that all who offer music to the public must give more attention to its quality. The phonograph operators also had the trump card of selectivity, of allowing the customer to choose the selection he pays for. But music operators cannot depend on the customers to grasp the value of selectivity in the midst of so much music. The phonograph trade must do more and more promotion, more advertising, more merchandising of the special advantages it offers in its music.

The flaw in the argument is obvious – the musically sophisticated public of 1948 found jukebox selections strictly limited. For example, Wurlitzer, Packard's *Pla-mor* and *Manhattan* were still offering 24 selections. Seeburg and Rock-ola were offering only 20 (with the latter vehemently asserting that this was quite sufficient). Filben improved the score with 30, while Aireon and AMI offered 48 and 40 selections respectively, although this was achieved by playing both A and B sides. It was obvious that this limited selection would not save the jukebox.

In the wider sense, 1948 was a year of bad news. There was talk that America could go to war against Russia, while labour relations and the economy were in bad shape. James Ceasar Petrillo, the boss of the musicians union (whose battles with the jukebox industry had caused a ban on his members making records during the war years which was only lifted on the personal appeal of President Roosevelt who argued that music was an essential morale-booster) resumed his fight when peace deflated the patriotism argument. The ban on new recordings was resumed. Furthermore, it seemed increasingly likely that copyright laws would be amended to put a royalty tax on jukebox music. Nevertheless two separate events occurred which gave a foretaste of a brighter future. One was the short-lived appearance of the Filben *Maestro*, whose dynamic styling pointed the way to the 1950s. The other, which was destined to save the jukebox, was paradoxically a major development in background music, for many the chief threat to the industry.

*Below and Right Massive faceted plastics borrowed from the Wurlitzer 1100 and the unique cobra's head grille motif show the Filben **Maestro** to be a product of the forties. Even so, its button bank and aggressive lines indicate the shape of things to come.*

Chapter Five

'Gee Dad, its a Wurlitzer'

It is likely that the antipathy of the Jukebox trade to background music blinkered it to the salvation offered by the introduction of Seeburg's Select-o-Matic *200* Library system in March 1948. As well as offering AM-FM radio, a PA system and a tape recorder, this device had a 200-selection (100 disc) changer system. All these features were contained in one cabinet, which included the facility for programming using a pre-set timer, for transmitting via telephone lines, for operating and controlling the volume remotely, and for selecting any record in any order.

Looking back one wonders how the jukebox world could have been so blind to the obvious fact that this could indeed be the jukebox of the future. Seeburg themselves obviously kept quiet – after all, they still had the 20-selection *Model 148* 'Trashcan' to sell! Seeburg described it as 'The most brilliant achievement in Commercial Music.' No-one could have been in any doubt that it would change the course of jukebox history. The mechanisms previously used, some of which had their roots in the pioneer days, were instantly obsolete. The *Select-o-matic* was a masterpiece of compact precision engineering. Radically innovative, playing either 10 inch or 12 inch 78 rpm discs vertically but using only a single tone arm, it was the result of research that started before the war. The newness of the mechanism was matched by the cabinet styling. For the first time since the 1930s the mechanism was exposed to view, despite Seeburg's 1946 statement that: 'The time is past when the public is entertained by watching a selector mechanism. Musical taste and public discrimination have advanced, and as the novelty of coin-operated phonographs has worn off, there is more and more insistence on quality music reproduction.' Those sentiments clearly did not last long because the new mechanism with its transverse action spanned the entire width of the machine, on full view under a simple curved glass reminiscent of a display case. The casework was of striking, striped wood with sharp angles, and the grill of simple chrome plated strips that picked up the reflections of a concealed, animated colour-screen.

Designed by Nils Miller, the jukebox matched the move towards 'Swedish Modern', a term first heard at the 1939 World's Fair. Progressive Americans were quick to buy modern Swedish furniture

ONLY SEEBURG
HAS THE
Select-o-matic 100
MECHANISM

The Select-O-Matic "100" mechanism... the most revolutionary development for the playing of recorded music since the invention of the phonograph... has established new standards of performance for coin-operated music.

Only the Select-O-Matic "100" Mechanism—world's first commercial mechanism designed exclusively for the playing of 45 RPM records—plays records in the vertical position, never drops a record, never turns one over. Vertical play means greater sales appeal through increased public interest. And, when records are stored and played in the vertical position dust, dirt, and abrasives do not settle in the grooves, thereby increasing both record and stylus life.

Beyond this, the performance of the Select-O-Matic "100" has proved it to be the most efficient operating mechanism ever incorporated in a coin-operated music system.

Page 8

Above Seeburg's select-o-matic mechanism was a unique piece of precision engineering which made other jukeboxes old-fashioned overnight.

in the immediate post-war period, partly because of its instant availability, the result of Sweden's neutrality during World War II. Swedish Modern, synonymous with the latest in furniture design, was an appropriate new look for this jukebox given Seeburg's Swedish origins and close cultural links with the country. Furthermore, the fact that Seeburg had developed this jukebox was reassuring to the trade. The company's impeccable reputation for quality and sound engineering gave much needed credibility following the high mortality rate of bright new hopes. As the trade press commented: 'This manufacturer not only is one of the major coin phonograph producers of the country, but was a pioneer in the fine instrument production of the early days, having produced pipe organs, pianos, and mechanical orchestration systems and pacing the industry in coin phonographs since the return of such equipment along with Repeal in 1934'.

This quantum leap in the design of the *Select-o-Matic* which doubled or quadrupled a jukebox's capacity instantly made such machines a viable proposition again. Its other strength was in having a wide selection of discs, offering music for various occasions, ranging from mellow mid-afternoon gatherings to the nightime crowd. The jukebox industry, or at least those operators who had signed up with Seeburg, could now face with renewed confidence the threat which had looked set to exterminate the American jukebox.

Yet, before the industry became too self-

Above and below The Chantal **Meteor 200** *ranks as one of the most uniquely styled of all jukeboxes. Unfortunately, as the new wave of American manufacturers who sprang up after the war discovered, most operators preferred to deal with established names.*

satisfied, it had to act. It had to follow in Seeburg's footsteps by increasing disc selection and improving its styling, which had too often been an old-fashioned cosmetic package. The value of the *Select-o-Matic* was that it balanced mechanism and styling, or form and function. The problem this posed for the competition became obvious when Joseph Clements, in the difficult position of taking over from Paul Fuller whose style had given Wurlitzer its identity, aped the new cabinet layout while retaining the traditional Wurlitzer theatrical look. Not only was the *Model 1250* a regressive step after the compact *1100*, but an inconsistent one. And the result was a comparatively cumbersome design. Wurlitzer did however double its selection by enabling both sides of the record to be played, using two tone arms, yet the whole machine reeked of compromise, even to the extent that on examination there are indications that Wurlitzer had hoped initially to make the *1250* a 60-selection machine. These weaknesses should not, though, invalidate the jukebox entirely. To many, the Seeburg must have seemed too clinical and design orientated, while the *1250* had the advantage of being faithful to the tradition of jukebox glamour.

With the eventful 1940s in the past, the industry was reconciled to the jukebox having lost its unique character. The beginning of a new decade also put a spotlight on social changes which put their stamp on the 1950s. The most significant, for the jukebox, was its new status as a symbol of the American way of life for the rest of the world, which seemed mesmerised by pop culture, particularly films, television and music. The American influence dominated Europe both culturally and economically – the Marshall Plan was pumping seventeen billion dollars into putting Europe back on its feet. Outside the USA many were seeing American products, including jukeboxes, for the first time. And the most dramatic example of the jukebox symbolising American culture and new industrial design was the inclusion of the Seeburg 'Trashcan', in the display of American goods and industrial products at the Japan Trade Exhibition held in Yokohama in 1949.

While America was receptive to European and Japanese influences, the rest of the world was equally interested in what had been termed the 'Coca-Cola Culture'. The growth of a world market, which prior to the war had been in its infancy, had a drastic effect on the American jukebox industry.

Not only were sales of new products enhanced, but more importantly an outlet was provided for second-hand equipment. This meant that American operators could change over their models increasingly rapidly. Indigenous jukebox industries too were spawned in other countries. The results were varied, ranging from the good to the bad and the positively ugly. On that score Seeburg had no need to worry; the company was still calling the shots.

Towards the end of the 1940s vinyl records began to appear, and although the majority of discs were still 78 rpm singles, new technology allowing for closer grooves resulted in the 33⅓ LP which Columbia introduced in 1948. This was designed for, and gave further impetus to, the growing home entertainment and background music markets. It was closely followed by the next stage in the modern record, the 7 inch 45 rpm record which RCA launched in 1949. Seeburg was in close co-operation with RCA, who accepted the point which had been frequently made by the jukebox trade, that jukeboxes were a major factor in making discs into hits. Previously the jukebox manufacturers had felt that the record companies had not given them

The introduction of the 45 rpm record meant Seeburg was in the unique position of having the only system, the 100B (above), which could handle the seven inch disc, although other makes as well as Seeburg's own 100A could be adapted from the ten inch 78 rpm to the new discs. Seeburg also introduced the first one hundred selection wallbox (right), which was to be used, either with a jukebox or a 'hideaway' unit so extensively through the fifties that it is now regarded as an essential element of 'diner art'.

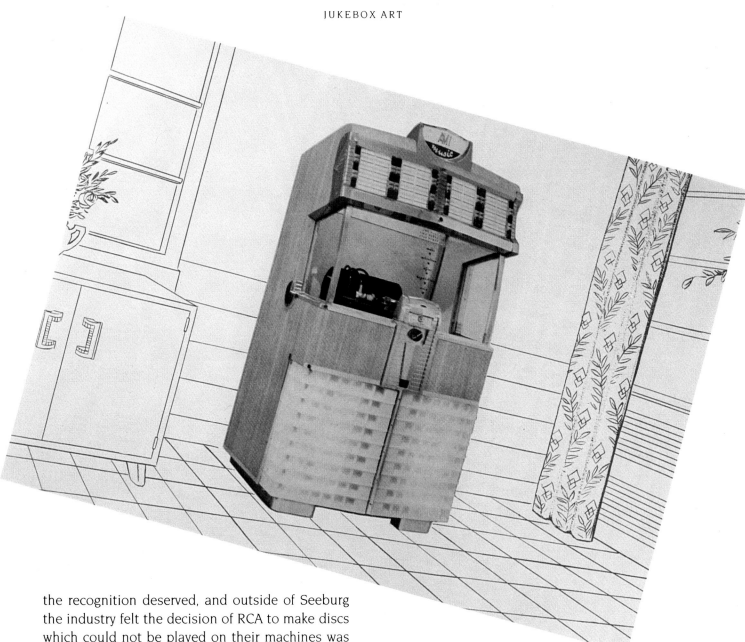

The AMI E was, in many ways, a transitional stage between forties and fifties style. The chunky lower plastics change colour with turning cylinders in the forties' tradition, but the clean cabinet lines led naturally into the successful F and G models.

the recognition deserved, and outside of Seeburg the industry felt the decision of RCA to make discs which could not be played on their machines was another chapter in its decline.

There was small consolation when the truth was revealed. Seeburg unveiled its 1950 Model *100B* (superficially a scaled down *100A*) which played the new 45 rpm discs! To pacify those who had only recently bought the *100A*, Seeburg had a programme for converting it to 45 rpm. But existence of three record speeds did now have enormous consequences. Columbia was marketing a record player to accommodate 33⅓ rpm discs (with record sales topping one million in the first year), concentrating on home entertainment so successfully that other record companies were also obliged to bring out 33⅓ discs, including RCA which was marketing a record player for the 45 rpms. Pop music singles were also beginning to be divided, with records aimed at an affluent mainly white audience being increasingly available on 45s, while 78s were aimed at people who were not buying new record players. At this time the record manufacturers, shops, and

radio stations were explicit in their racial categorisation of music. This was to have drastic social consequences for the jukebox.

The musical strands of jump R & B, western swing and hillbilly which had become popular during the 1940s began to fuse into embryonic rock'n'roll giving teenagers, who had at the same time been emerging as a distinct social group, their own music. In fact the teenager had been a major user of the jukebox – or the jive crate – through the 1940s. (Wurlitzer's advertisements portraying elegant society in evening dress gathered round the jukebox were more an indication of the trades craving for respectability than reality.) Now, however, the teenage market was becoming increasingly affluent. Although the industry pretended to ignore this factor (not until 1956 did teenagers appear in promotional material with the Seeburg *KD*), the jukebox was inextricably linked with teenagers and rock'n'roll through the whole of the 1950s. But as the jukebox became the prime source of rock'n'roll it found itself a target.

In 1956 the following report was published.

Birmingham – rock'n'roll was blasted here last week by the White Citizen's Council, which has started a campaign to rid all jukeboxes of rock'n'roll platters. Local coin machine operators said the plan was 'fantastic' and that they had not yet been contacted by the Council. However, Asa (Ace) Carter, executive secretary of the North Alabama Council, speaking at a rally here last week, charged that the rock and roll music – the current rage of the southern white teenager – was inspired by the National Association for the Advancement of Coloured People and other pro-integration

*Although Hawtins was a large concern, its first (**Victory** style) **Music Maker** showed the limitations in its styling. Most, if not all original **Music Makers** were subsequently re-housed in the new **MKII** cabinet.*

forces. Carter indicated that the Council will publicize the name of any operator who refuses to ban what Carter called 'immoral' records.

To their credit the jukebox operators did not bow to this pressure. This quotation has been singled out for the explicitness of its message, but there were countless moves by various groups nationwide throughout the fifties to ban rock'n'roll from jukeboxes and radio, either on racial grounds or those of 'juvenile delinquency'.

The new impetus that the Seeburg *100B*, brought to jukeboxes put other manufacturers out on a limb, even those whose mechanisms could be adapted to play 45s, were still stuck with few selections and old-fashioned styling. By the time they caught up with the latest developments Rockola with the 1952 *Fireball 1436*, Wurlitzer with the 1954 *Model 1700*, and AMI with the 1954 *Model 'E'* (though AMI continued to offer 78 rpm as an option) – Seeburg had made itself the name of the decade. Of all the companies, however, AMI was in

the best position to survive the transitional period of the early 1950s. It was actively engaged in export, and also had a policy of selling its mechanisms and amplifiers as separate units to other manufacturers. In addition, AMI officially supplied troops during the Korean War, having priority access to raw materials when other jukebox manufacturers were rationed.

One particularly important market for AMI was Britain. Although Britain's post-war economy was in a poor state there was a massive government drive to regenerate industry, which culminated in the 1946 'Britain can make it' exhibition of new products. With raw materials in short supply, and a population still suffering wartime rationing priority was given to much needed export revenue rather

The G carried on with much of the same lines, although with a new X-type mechanism it could also offer two hundred selections.

AMI enlivened their cabinets with an amazing choice of colours, in accord with the contemporary craze for anything from cars to refrigerators being offered in colour choices.

than the home market. The exception was entertainment, with the authorities realising this was an important morale-booster. A direct consequence was Hawtins version of the Wurlitzer *Victory*, using a Wurlitzer simplex mechanism under licence. In fact Wurlitzer had already appeared in Britain before the war but now, like other American manufacturers, suffered because the post-war import restrictions excluded their products.

An operator, Thomas Kash – who had dealt with Wurlitzer before the war and in 1943 was co-patentee of a modification to the Simplex mech-

The AMI F machine was characterised by robust, basic construction which made it a particular favourite in the export market.

anism went into production in 1946 modernising pre-war Wurlitzers. Initially he handled the pre-war American light-up conversions, but later new and quite elaborate cabinets were built incorporating old mechanisms. As well as patenting several jukebox improvements his company KEB made a jukebox utilising AMI mechanisms. The fact that AMI was prepared to supply the individual elements of its jukeboxes enabled another British company, Balfour Engineering, to import some parts, with the remainder (including the cabinet, amplifiers and speaker) representing a sufficiently high percentage of the finished product to satisfy the Board of Trade that its jukeboxes could be described as British made.

The majority of AMI's in Britain were these hybrids (*Bal-Amis*). Though some model *Es* (1953) came over with American cabinets, the *Bal-Ami* was

THE INCOMPARABLE AMI MODEL "F-120"

based on the 1956 *Model G 80*. Bal-Ami's most popular model was the 40-selection machine, whose small scale suited cafes and the recent phenomenon of coffee bars. The latter (distinguished by modern decor stylish furniture and an expresso coffee machine) with dance halls, represented the few social centres specifically for teenagers, with the jukebox being their main source of rock'n'roll (such music was all but excluded from the BBC, which had a monopoly of radio broadcasting).

In 1958 Bal-Ami brought out its own design, a petite simplified version of the *Model H*, called the *Super-Forty*. Lacking the grandeur and massive chrome and glass of the American original (as well as short-changing on the number of selections offered) this little British jukebox, like the Ameri-

Left The AMI H of 1957 was a radical departure from the E and F series, showing the influence of auto-styling in its big wrap-round glass screen.

*Above The scaled down British version of AMI's **Model H** was a coffee bar favourite. Holding only 20 records, the **Super 40** was the luxury version of the Bal-AMI **Junior** which was a similarly scaled down G. Unlike other Bal-Amis the **Super 40** featured a specially designed mechanism.*

can inspired cars and singers of the time, came straight out of toy town. Even more bizarre machines occurred with AMI's other European licensee, Jensen Musik of Denmark. Inspired by the aesthetics of Scandinavian Modern, this company housed the AMI mechanism in blatant copies of the Seeburg *M100A – M100B* style. These Danish (IMA-AMI) jukeboxes enjoyed a good reputation for quality from 1953–57. In 1956 however the Seeburg style was dropped in favour of the American AMI *G*. And in 1957 the classic line of the AMI *H* were the victim of the Europeans, appearing in the IMA-AMI, a strangely mutant machine which parodied rather than echoed the styling of the original.

Rock-ola was also involved in joint efforts in Europe, though retaining strict control over its image by supplying an essentially complete juke-box, leaving only the amplifier, speaker junction box, and wiring to be made locally. Externally these Rock-olas, made in conjunction with Nova Auto-mat of Hamburg, differ only from the American version in their cabinet finish. Neither Wurlitzer nor

*AMI followed the **H** with a simplified cabinet in the **Model I**. It retained the main style of the **H** but dropped the front light bar which had been such a distinctive feature.*

*The Danish **IMA-AMI** was a strange hybrid, with an AMI mechanism housed in cabinets which were almost exact copies of Seeburgs!*

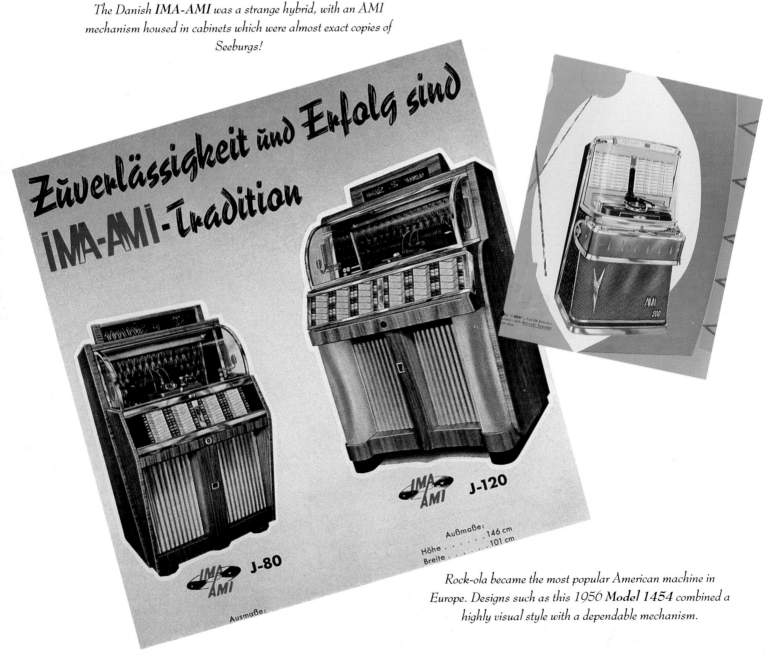

*Rock-ola became the most popular American machine in Europe. Designs such as this 1956 **Model 1454** combined a highly visual style with a dependable mechanism.*

Seeburg made any concessions to foreign markets, apart from Hawtin's use of the simplex mechanism. Having produced the *Victory* style machine, the company introduced a fresh model in 1949, called the *Music Maker MKII* in a new cabinet. Publicity claimed it was the work of a leading industrial designer (unfortunately without saying who), and its simple lines like those of the Mills *Constellation* evoke the aesthetics of contemporary industrial design. The *Music Maker* was then taken over by another British company, Ditchburn, which operated and manufactured it. The *Music Maker* survived into the mid-1950s when the relaxation of trade restrictions allowed both American and continental European machines to be imported.

The indigenous European machines, with a few notable exceptions, were generally derivative of the Americans. For example *NSM*, destined to become a major international jukebox, owed its style to the influence of Seeburg and Wurlitzer, while its lower price gave the Euro-machine the advantage. Eventually Ditchburn stopped manufacturing the *Music Maker* in favour of the eccentric but stylish German made *Telematic*, which offered increased selections (100 compared to the *Music Maker*'s 16) and modernised most of them by chopping the cabinet and topping it with a fibre-glass and plastic canopy to give it modern lines, as well as increasing the selections to 30. These were advertised as low-budget machines and looked particularly dowdy compared with Ditchburn's latest import, the *Telematic 200*. As well as manufacturing background music systems Ditchburn was a big operator with sites including USAF bases in Britain. After suffering the sarcastic comments of the American servicemen, who saw Ditchburn's products as yet

Above *Although the new Ditchburn **MkII** was housed in a stylish cabinet, its mechanism was still essentially pre-war Wurlitzer.*

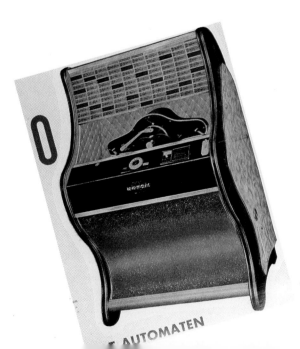

Left *The **Telematic 200** featured a front grille bathed in moving, coloured light as well as an unusual serpentine cabinet.*

Above The American inspiration for many European jukeboxes is clearly demonstrated by comparing the Seeburg **L100** of 1957 with the **'Harmonie'**.

Below The restyled **Telematic 200** featured panoramic styling which showed the influence of AMI's wrap-round screen. Although these German machines were more sophisticated than Ditchburn's own products, the Company stopped importing them in favour of the radical Seeburg **222** in 1959.

another example of olde-worlde Britain, the company began importing Seeburgs. Furthermore, Wurlitzers began to appear alongside the *Bal Ami H* and models that were essentially the same as the American originals.

Despite this there was a last British attempt on the jukebox market (although there have been some more recent successes) – the uniquely styled *Chantal Meteor*. This 200-selection machine was launched at the end of 1958 using a mechanism which, like the cabinet styling, was alien to anything seen before or since. The origins of this mechanism were clouded in cloak-and-dagger secret meetings, but it seems that the consortium formed to produce the machine had been sold a dud. Although the consortium had a background of

aircraft engineering and had sufficient expertise to convert the original design into a viable mechanism, it lacked experience in jukeboxes. The first machines were unreliable and suffered from sound distortion. Even worse, people quickly worked out that a cigarette burn in the plastic dome meant a knitting needle could be inserted through the hole to give a free play. Ironically, not long after these

*Below The Seeburg **G** and **W** were a pair of almost identical machines, the difference being that the de-luxe **G** featured chrome pilasters whilst those of the **W** were fibreglass, the first use of this material in a jukebox.*

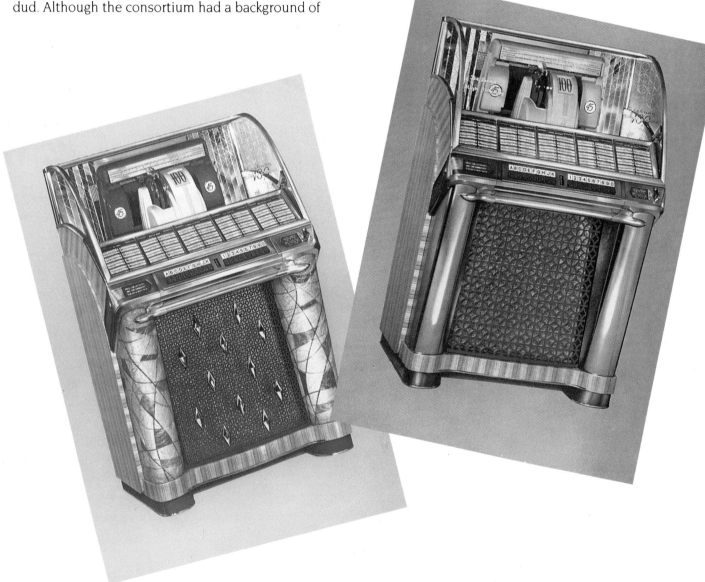

*Right The Seeburg **C** dropped the Scandinavian look in a return to the forties image of bright, decorative styling — even to the extent of reviving the idea of coloured turning cylinders in the pilasters.*

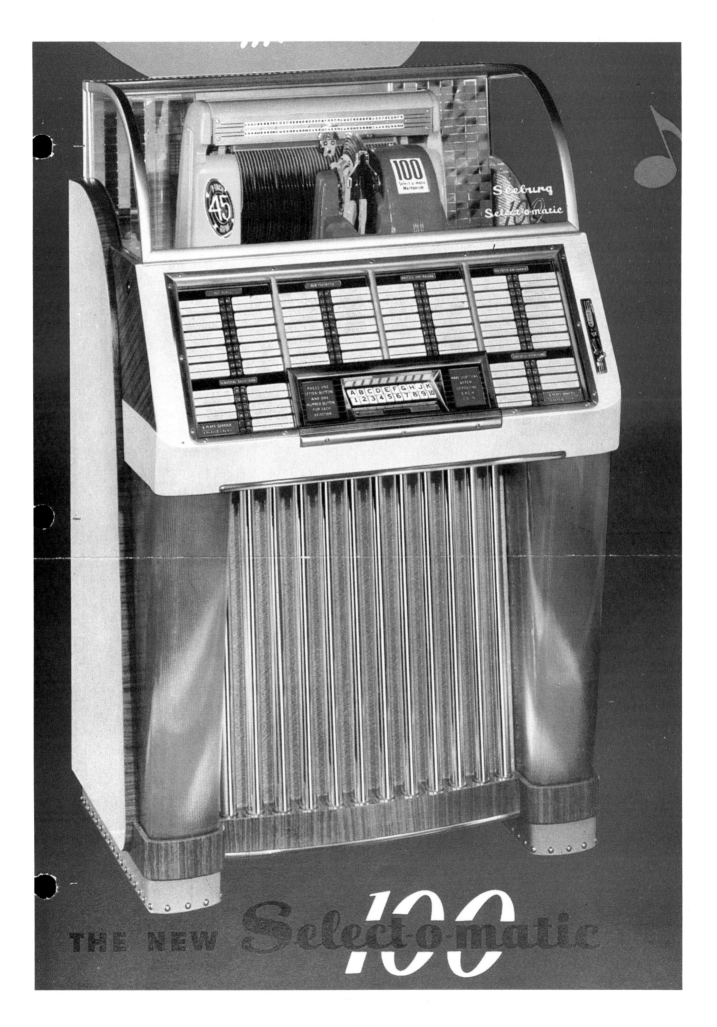

major problems were rectified and the *Chantal* gained limited success, the factory burnt down!

Although production resumed after this 1960-setback Chantal discovered, as had others before, that a revolutionary new design and production difficulties were a fatal combination. Operating problems (the record loading was difficult, awkward to move, and its design made it unsuitable for many sites) too heavily weighed against high-tech style. And, in the end, profits began to suffer. Modern collectors and enthusiasts may now appreciate the fine styling but in their day jukeboxes stood or fell not on how they looked but on how much revenue they earned.

The designs of 1950s jukeboxes mirror the events of that decade perfectly. From the 100B at the beginning, there existed exactly the same dilemma that occurred in American design generally – striking a balance between aesthetic ideals and the public's perception. A 1953 Dutch report on American design commented that 'American industry

*Below For 1954 Seeburg's **HF100R** introduced the 'bandshell' (cantilevered) top which was subsequently adopted by other manufacturers.*

*Right and details The Seeburg **V200** was the first two hundred selection jukebox. Its sophisticated new technology was housed in an imposing cabinet and both the changer and the revolving title drum were covered by an enormous curved glass screen. In many ways this was the last 'real' Seeburg – after this model the firm ceased to be a family business.*

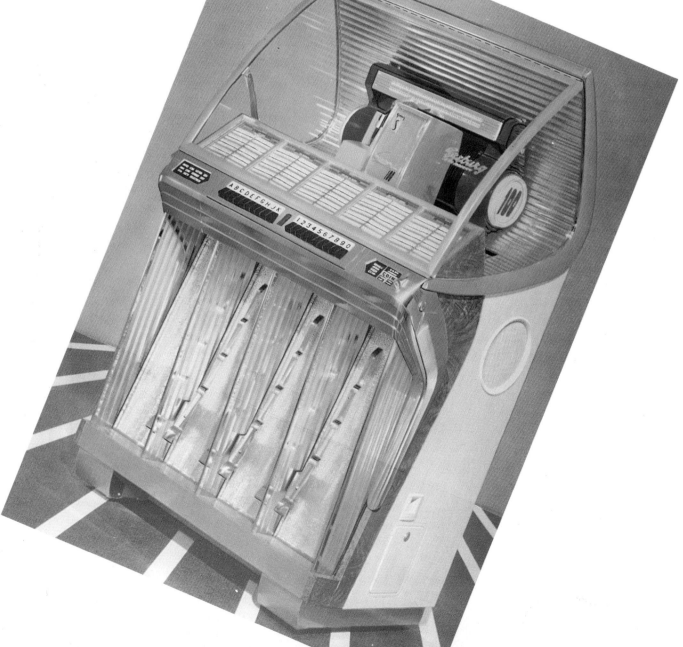

often compels the designer to concessions tending to what, not without reason, we habitually call "bad taste". Fortunately for jukeboxes teenagers rather than museum curators were the ultimate test, and the deliberate obsolescence factor that character-ised the American consumer economy until about 1956 was not a major handicap. The pace was set by the major force in the doctrine of conspicuous consumerism, the automobile industry, whose chief design guru, Harley Earl had the design philosophy 'go all the way and then back off a little'.

The latest ideas in jukebox style ironically meant that everything from the *Aireon* to the *100B* was considered an aberration, so the industry reverted to the old styling and marketing wars within a framework of common aesthetics. Even Seeburg became decorative with the 1952 *Model C* returned to the coloured light turning cylinders of the 1940s, the 1953 model sported decorative illuminated fibre glass pillasters, and the 1954 *Model HF 100R* featured chrome-plated festoons cascading down its front grill. But in no way do these decorative elements detract from the jukebox's style. instead they act as a reminder of Wurlitzer's adage that showmanship was an essential element of the jukebox. In any event Seeburg's cabinet styling set the pace for Rock-ola and Wurlitzer, with Rock-ola's 1953 *Comet-fireball* in particular showing this influence.

The major jukebox breakthrough conveniently occurred in 1955, thereby neatly dividing the last decade of the great jukebox years. Again, it was Seeburg's technology which set the pace with the most impressive of all the 1950s classics, the mighty *V 200*. The first *200* selection jukebox, it also introduced a new technology – dual pricing and the tormat memory which registered selections electronically. The importance of the former was that the recently introduced EP disc, playing twice as long as the single, was uneconomical for the jukebox operator when there was no way of getting the customer to pay for extra playtime. Extending the concept of the *100A* that the jukebox should be a library of records, Seeburg favoured the EP because it extended the musical range available on singles. Dual pricing allowed both kinds of disc to be installed on the same machine, with 15 cents

Two Hundred

"COME BACK WHEN YOU GROW UP"
BOBBY VEE
"SWANEE RIVER..."

"THE DOOR IS STILL OPEN TO MY HEART"
☆ DEAN MARTIN ☆
"EVERY MINUTE, EVERY HOUR"

"HUNG ON YOU"
☆ THE RIGHTEOUS BROS. ☆
"UNCHAINED MELODY"
PHILLES 129

"MY MAN"
☆ BARBRA STREISAND ☆
"WHERE IS THE WONDER"
COLUMBIA 43323

"MOONLIGHT AND ROSES"
☆ VIC DANA ☆
"WHAT'LL I DO"
DOLTON 309

"PEOPLE GOT TO BE FREE"
THE RASCALS
"MY WORLD"

"THE ARENA"
☆ AL HIRT ☆
"YESTERDAY"
RCA VICTOR 8736

"TRULY, TRULY, TRUE"
☆ BRENDA LEE ☆
"I STILL MISS SOMEONE"
DECCA 31762

"MY LOVE, FORGIVE ME"
☆ ROBERT GOULET ☆
"I'D RATHER BE RICH"
COLUMBIA 43131

"IT'S A SIN TO TELL A LIE"
☆ TONY BENNETT ☆
"A TASTE OF HONEY"
COLUMBIA 43073

10¢

Hit Tune

SINGLE TUNE
PER SELECTION
3 SINGLES ▸ QUARTER 10¢

RHYTHM and BLUES

FOLK and WESTERN

Selections

SINGLE TUNE
SELECTION

"YOU DON'T HEAR"
KITTY WELLS
"SIX LONELY HOURS"

"I'VE GOT RHYTHM"
THE HAPPENINGS
"YOU'RE IN A BAD WAY"

"HEROES & VILLAINS"
☆ THE BEACH BOYS ☆
"YOU'RE WELCOME"
THE BROTHERS 1001

"MAKE ME YOUR BABY"
☆ BARBARA LEWIS ☆
"LOVE TO BE LOVED"
ATLANTIC 2300

"KING OF THE ROAD
ROGER MILLER
"ATTA BOY, GIRL"
SMASH 1965

R2
C2
D2
E2
F2
G2
H2
J2
K2

M2
N2
P2
Q2
R2
S2
T2
U2
V2

"YAKETY ORGAN"
LENNY DEE
"A WALK IN THE BLACK FOREST"

"TWO FOR THE ROAD"...Vocal
HENRY MANCINI & HIS ORCH.
"HAPPY BAREFOOT BOY"
RCA VICTOR 9200

"THE WORLD WE KNEW" (Over & Over)
☆ FRANK SINATRA ☆
"YOU ARE THERE"
REPRISE 0610

"LOVE MAKES THE WORLD GO 'ROUND"
☆ DEON JACKSON ☆
"YOU SAID YOU LOVED ME"
CARLA 2526

"A LITTLE BIT OF HEAVEN"
☆ RONNIE DOVE ☆
"IF I LIVE TO BE A HUNDRED"
DIAMOND 184

ALL-TIME FAVORITES

the price of an EP, 10 cents for a single.

Meanwhile Wurlitzer was trying to regain the status it had enjoyed in the 1940s. Since the *Model 1250* it had produced a variety of styles, all of which suffered from the restriction of an old-fashioned mechanism. The extent of these problems was demonstrated with the 1953 *Model 1500*, a magnificent, eccentric machine that increased the number of selections by using a double changer mechanism.

One year later, though, Wurlitzer introduced its successful carousel mechanism that gave the company a brighter future. A catchy slogan – 'Gee Dad, it's a Wurlitzer' – put the name back in the public consciousness. Liberated from the restrictions of the old-style mechanism, the *Model 1700* cabinet style showed little change from the previous *1600* and *1650s*, but the following year's *1800* showed a fresh, dynamic image made possible by the liberating effect of the new mechanism.

The
WURLITZER
Fourteen Fifty

WITH TEXTILEATHER COVERED CABI

Queenly consort for the Wurlitzer Fourteen Hundred, pictured on the page, the Fourteen Fifty plays any speed record—ten inch 78 RPM seven inch 45 or 33-1/3 RPM. Now you can use them all, and all on o Identical, in appearance, to the Fourteen Hundred in every respect but one handsomely housed in a wooden cabinet covered with Textileather. One of the furniture field, Textileather is scuff proof, water proof and alcohol proc mahogany or in blonde, blue and brown colors to compliment lo glamorous Textileather will last the life of the phe

As in the Fourteen Hundred, this model incorporates Zenith Cobra Sound System to bring out the glorious brilliance and the fine groove records, and to bring in the greatest flow of coins ever e

OPTIONAL COLORS

ng
3 LP;
ograph!
Fourteen Fifty is
materials in the fine
lable in standard
eriors, tough,

and the Dynatone
ons of the micro-
any phonograph.

Model 1450

Right and following pages Wurlitzer Model 1400 and
1450 were basically identical but offered in different cabinet
finishes, the 1400 being walnut, the 1450 'texileather'.

WURLITZER LEADS
IN VALUE

The
WURLITZER
Fourteen Hundred

B R I L L I A N T   N E W   S T Y L I N G

W A L N U T   C A B I N E T

Here it is! As rich as a king's ransom in beauty. As colorful as a coronation ceremony. Wurlitzer's crowning achievement—the Wurlitzer Fourteen Hundred! Equipped with Zenith Cobra Pick-ups and the famed Dynatone Sound System, it retains Wurlitzer's profit-proven record complement—48 tunes on 24 records. It introduces a new and sensational example of Wurlitzer leadership . . . *30 second changeover from 78 RPM to 45 or 33-1/3 RPM records!*

Feast your eyes on its completely visible, softly glowing, plexiglass record changer compartment! The background gleams with an iridescent eye-pleasing pattern of musical fantasy. Look at the brilliance of those pilasters! Illuminated color cylinders reflect their light through a pattern of molded diamonds to create a magical illusion of changing color. And to compliment it all—an exquisitely styled nickeled metal grille facade backed by an indestructible perforated metal speaker screen.

Proudly Wurlitzer presents the Fourteen Hundred. Its regal splendor assures a royal reception that will mean greater profits for you!

Model 1400

Right The Wurlitzer 1600/1650 was the last to use its traditional record stack mechanism.

Below The 1500/1550 (like its predecessor offered in a choice of cabinet finish) featured twin record stacks in a desperate attempt to increase selections by doubling the mechanism.

With the **Model 1700** Wurlitzer finally caught up with its competition by having a new mechanism designed expressly for seven inch records.

Right Views like these of **1800s** being produced in Wurlitzer's factory only hint at the large volume production in which the industry was engaged.

Blick in das
Overather Betriebswerk

Fordern Sie den Prospekt der neuartigen Tanzkugel (als Bundesgebrauchsmuster

eingetragen) für Tanzbars und Säle, zu jedem Modell passend, unverbindlich an

1956 was an important year for Wurlitzer it was one hundred years from the time Rudolph had rented a small room in Cincinnati as his first store. Since there had been little to celebrate since the 1940s Wurlitzer (a household name since the turn of the century) ensured this 'birthday' would be memorable. It launched a special commemorative jukebox, the *Centennial*, which was appropriately one of the most distinctive machines of the era. Wurlitzer also gave nationwide parties accompanied by promotional competitions and publicity.

The 'poor relation' *Centennial Model 1900* offered 104 selections, but in answer to Seeburg's *V 200* the 'real' *Centennial*, the *2000*, was the pièce de résistance. Part of the title display took the form of animated books whose pages turned at the press of a button. The following year's models continued this idea, but although their styling changes were minor the effect was to coarsen the classic *Centennial* look. By this time America's consumer society, which had been on a roller coaster of conspicuous buying, was suffering from a mild recession while becoming increasingly conscious that the worst excesses of planned obsolescence were resulting in inferior products. Commentators and newspaper

Above The carousel mechanism allowed Wurlitzer to celebrate its hundredth anniversary with the 1956 **Centennial 2000** as its first two hundred selection machine. A novelty feature were the 'turning pages', a device which allowed the extra titles to be displayed without blocking the view of the changer. At the push of a button, pages of two blocks would turn over to show the titles. The **Model 1900 Centennial** lacked the novelty of the 2000's turning pages, and was offered as an economy model.

Above Raymond Loewy returned to jukeboxes with the 1957 **United**. His brief was to design a Jukebox that was visually attractive but serviceable.

Right The **Centennial** look was continued with the next year's 2100, which featured a re-styled front grille and top castings.

EBURG *two hundred*

o new Seeburg phonographs are rare combi-
of beauty, functional design, programming
ons and construction features that will assure
ximum earning potential from every location.

The new Seeburg Two Hundred has the ul-
timate in distinguishing features including the straight-
in-line Select-O-Matic mechanism...Dual Pricing...
new Dual Programming...Tormat Memory Unit.

Left and Above *First introduced with the K.D., automobile-style fins embellishing the front grille remained a feature of the next year's models, the 161 (one hundred and sixty selections) and the two hundred selection model 201 of 1958.*

Below and Right *Having set the pace for new technology in the late forties, Seeburg continued to be responsible for innovation through the fifties. The Model 222 (right) was the first stereo jukebox and came supplied with test records and detailed instructions as to the positioning of auxiliary speakers in order to attain true stereo sound.*

EREOPHONIC

WITH CHANNEL 2

eophonic records are played
they bring all the new brilliance, depth, realism and spa-
ciousness of this wonderful new
recording method to every location. When nonaural records
are played they sound better
than ever before.
Note, too, the dynamic,
modern beauty of the cabinet.
Channel 1 and Channel 2 have
been separated to create a vis-
l as well as auditory image
stereophonic music.

Seeburg Wall-O-Matics extend the
value of stereo, dual programming
and dual pricing. They are available
in three different types to meet the
requirements of every location. Attractive, streamlined chromium-
plated housing. 3-wire type for simple, quick installation.

.. SEE Seeburg Stereo
'g Distributor

**THE NEW
SEEBURG "220"**

specifications
100 Selections. Single Pricing.
Height—55¼"; Width—32½"; Depth—27".
Weight (Net)—334 lbs.; Weight (Ship.)—384 lbs.
Audio Power Output—36 Watts (18 Watts per Channel)

articles were beginning to criticise ostentation, and America began to look again at European styles of cars and domestic appliances which were being marketed with increasing success. Although the massive automobile industry put its head in the sand, continuing to produce the style which Raymond Loewy had branded the 'jukebox on wheels', other industries took note, and the post 1957 jukebox is noticeably less opulent.

In 1957 Loewy, spokesman and one of the instigators of American industrial design, returned to jukeboxes, designing the *United*. As with his earlier work, the *Aireon* of the 1940s, the *United* failed to make any real effect on the jukebox world. Nevertheless, it is interesting that jukebox history should twice feature Loewy's work. By a neat irony Seeburg, who had traditionally disdained gimmicky styling, embellished the otherwise innovative hard-

Left The AMI K was the last of a series which had now lost its original design purpose. By 1960 jukeboxes, like the cars whose design fortunes they had often shared, were toning down for a new decade and a new image.

Right and above AMI's fiftieth anniversary model, the J, was the penultimate in a line of distinctive auto-style machines.

The AMI **Continental** of 1960 showed a dramatic rejection of the auto-styling which had characterised the *H* through to *K* series. The wrap-round title display enabled the changer (on view under a glass bubble) and the selector buttons to be uncluttered. The same cabinet style was used again the following year in the **Continental 2**.

edged cabinet design of the *KD* model with automobile-type fins, complete with stop lights – exactly the sort of feature Loewy always criticised in car design!

The last major influence on the 1950s jukebox was the advent of stereo, although the only way a jukebox could produce true stereo was through extension speakers (Seeburg issued meticulous instructions on how to set this up, complete with audio test records). The important factor was marketing. In an age when consumers constantly expected improved technology 'progress' was crucial – even if it was rooted more in hype than reality. Seeburg styled their first stereo, the 1959 *Model 222*, in order to emphasise the new sound, dividing the front grill into two distinct panels marked channel 1 and 2 In style it was heading straight for the 1960s.

AMI, meanwhile, was ending the decade on a high note, celebrating its fiftieth anniversary with a special anniversary model. The 1959 *Model J* was the penultimate of a series of auto-style AMI, whose characteristic large wrap-round glass screens and massed chrome derived from Detroit. But the end of the line, the toned-down 1960 K, looked as old-fashioned as the cars that had influenced it. The AMI style had been echoed in Rock-ola's *Tempos* of 1959 and 1960 (the latter, which was its silver anniversary model, being stereo). They too carried the look into the early sixties with updated versions the last of which was the 1962 *Empress*.

It was almost as if the big four – Wurlitzer, AMI, Seeburg and Rock-ola – who had together made the American jukebox, had responded together to a change in American society, for Wurlitzer too ended the decade with its last dynamic shape, the 1959 *Model 2300*. The following year Kennedy's electoral campaign finally laid to rest the popular

*Right The Rock-ola **Tempo II** embellished the previous model's design with a popular boomerang motif and introduced stereo sound. This styling was continued with the **Regis** and **Empress** models, by which time the auto-style image which had seemed so right for the original **Tempo** was looking decidedly dated.*

124

Left *Just before Wurlitzer closed its doors for the last time in 1974, bringing to an end a chapter in jukebox history, it produced the model* **1050** *(1973). Appropriately named the* **Nostalgia**, *it sought to re-capture the spirit of its forties triumphs. More recently, Deutsche Wurlitzer, who have kept Wurlitzer's name alive in its country of origin, have successfully marketed a reproduction of the classic model* **1015**.

THE **ROCK-OLA** Empress...
new all-purpose stereophonic-monaural phonograph
120 or 200 Selections

stereo

ROCK-OLA
REGIS
Model 1488

The World's Most Distinguished Phonograph

Above *Seeburg had already lost the fifties look with the* **222** *or, arguably, as long ago as the* **KD** *of 1957. The obviously 'jukebox' look made its last appearances with the* **AQ** *of 1960, and the* **DS160** *of 1962, notable for its two externally mounted auxiliary speakers, which could be swivelled to bias the sound.*

125

image of the 1950s. 'Ask not what your country can do for you, but what you can do for your country.' Rock'n'roll was dead, and popular music watered down to the point where America was ready to accept its own, indigenous sounds regurgitated in European packaging in the form of the Beatles. Jukeboxes, like cars, also shed their unique American quality in favour of a less individual Euro-look. In 1962 Seeburg brought out a revolutionary new *Console* style, the *LPC1*. Technically innovative in that it could play either 45 rpm singles or 33⅓ rpm mini-LPs, it had a greater novelty in the cabinet design. The company responsible, Sundborg-Ferar Inc, received the American Institute of Architects' Industrial Arts award which set the standard for the next decade. Its clean lines are so devoid of any obvious period characteristics that it is often mistaken for a 1970's machine. Nevertheless, it poses the question 'Should jukebox manufacturers care about winning the approval of the American Institute of Architects?'

The jukebox did not die after 1962, but it reverted to the position that had been foreseen in the late 1940's – it became a music machine, co-existing with background music systems, neither projecting nor receiving any emotional relationship with its patrons. Throughout the 1950s it had been, to an extent, living on borrowed time. Fortunately this indian summer of jukebox history has left such lasting impressions that jukeboxes still strongly evoke nostalgic memories for many people. Moreover, many were built to such demanding mechanical standards that they survived their design obsolescence, and jukeboxes from the 1940s are still at work across the globe, flying the stars and stripes of American cultural imperialism long after their country of birth has relegated them to folk memory. At last many of these veterans are being brought back home, to be refurbished along with those who have silently slept out the intervening years in outhouses and basements. Lovingly restored and alive with music once again, they are still bringing magic to those for whom the jukebox will always have a special place in history.

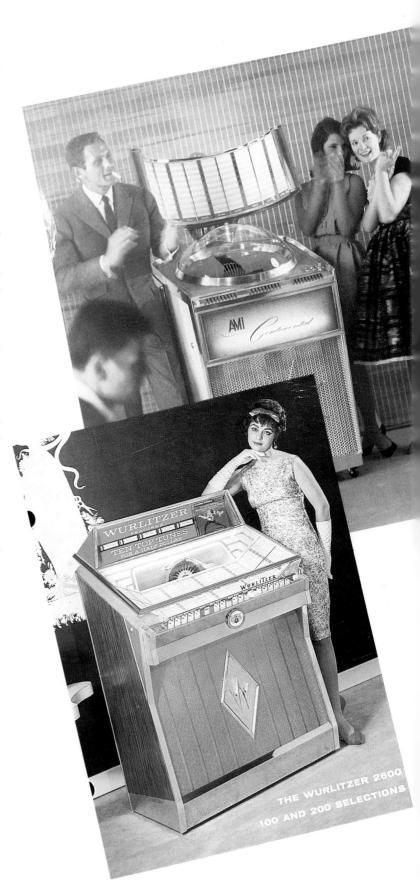

Above The Model 2400 of 1960 continued the trend which began with the Model 2300 of enclosing almost the entire mechanism within the title display. The following year's Model 2500 featured a distinctive cabinet, but by the 2600 of 1962 all traces of the glamour which had distinguished Wurlitzer through the years had gone.

Above *The Seeburg LPC1 of 1962 heralded a new era of jukebox style with its console-style cabinet. Seeburg, like the other manufacturers, were unsentimental about the jukebox, which had, to an extent, been living on borrowed time through the fifties. In the same way as had the 100A and 100B in the past, this new concept enabled the jukebox to move towards the future.*

Left *The Model 2300 was Wurlitzer's first stereo jukebox. By the end of the fifties the social climate in which the jukebox had thrived was coming to an end, and with it the special qualities of assurred styling also began to wane.*

Index